The Revolutionization of Chinese Youth

A Study of
Chung-kuo Ch'ing-nien

A publication of the
Center for Chinese Studies
University of California,
Berkeley, California 94720

Cover Colophon by Shih-hsiang Chen.

Center for Chinese Studies • CHINA RESEARCH MONOGRAPHS
UNIVERSITY OF CALIFORNIA, BERKELEY

/ NUMBER ONE

The Revolutionization of Chinese Youth

A Study of *Chung-kuo Ch'ing-nien*

JAMES R. TOWNSEND

Although the Center for Chinese Studies is responsible for the selection and acceptance of monographs in this series, responsibility for the opinions expressed in them and for the accuracy of statements contained in them rests with their authors.

Foreword

This publication initiates a new series of research monographs which will be published from time to time by the Center for Chinese Studies of the University of California at Berkeley.

Research on Communist China has made great progress, both in scope and in depth, during the past decade. It has produced a clear record of the major events of the period, and has advanced useful historical and sociological generalizations which contribute to the understanding of the Chinese revolution. American scholarship has played a leading role in much of this work, and the Center for Chinese Studies at Berkeley is pleased that it has been able to make some contribution.

Much, however, remains to be done. Nothing, it is probably safe to say, has more dramatically made this obvious than Mao Tse-tung's Great Proletarian Cultural Revolution. There is an urgent need for close, basic research on the structural problems of the Chinese Communist regime, and on the alternative policies that segments of the Chinese elite are trying to implement in order to solve or alleviate these problems. The Cultural Revolution reveals, if nothing more, that political forces continue to operate under the Chinese Communists, and that ideology and the heritage of the revolution are only inputs into a living, functioning political milieu.

The Center for Chinese Studies has undertaken this new series of monographs in recognition of the need for prompt reporting of research on Chinese Communist affairs, and in order to provide a medium for types of reports not readily available elsewhere. The series will include bibliographical aids and analyses, analytical studies of intermediate length, essays, and reports of investigations carried out under the Center's auspices. It will supplement, not replace, the series of book-length studies which the Center will continue to publish in collaboration with the University of California Press. It is particularly appropriate, in view of recent events, that this research monograph series starts with a study of the revolutionization of Chinese youth.

James R. Townsend is a member of the Department of Political Science in the University of California, Berkeley, and the author of a major analytical work on Chinese Communist political organization, *Political Participation in Communist China* (Center for Chinese Studies Books, No. 2, University of California Press, 1967). Professor Townsend spent the year 1966–67 in Hong Kong and much of the research for the present study was done from that vantage point. In addition to his teaching responsibilities, he is concurrently serving during 1967–68 as a research associate in the Center for Chinese Studies.

Professor Townsend's study reminds us of the fact, sometimes difficult of appreciation for outsiders studying the world's most long-lived civilization, that Chinese society has not only a past but also a future. The Center hopes that future monographs will attain the same high standard set for the series by Professor Townsend in this initial publication.

CHALMERS JOHNSON, *Chairman*
Center for Chinese Studies

Berkeley, California
September, 1967

Contents

7

AUTHOR'S ACKNOWLEDGMENTS

The Center for Chinese Studies at the University of California, Berkeley, provided financial assistance for research on this monograph during 1964–66. Additional research and writing were carried out in Hong Kong during 1966–67 under funds from a Rockefeller Foundation grant administered by the Department of Political Science at Berkeley. A portion of the monograph was presented as a paper for the Conference on the Microsocietal Study of the Chinese Political System, August 29–September 1, 1967, organized by the Subcommittee on Chinese Government and Politics of the Joint Committee on Contemporary China. I would like to acknowledge my debt to all of these organizations for their support, although I retain sole responsibility for the content of the study. I would also like to thank Ronald Ye-lin Cheng and Ru-fen Wang for research assistance on this project.

ABBREVIATIONS IN TEXT

CB   *Current Background*
CCP   Chinese Communist Party
CKCN   *Chung-kuo Ch'ing-nien*
CKCNP   *Chung-kuo Ch'ing-nien Pao*
CNA   *China News Analysis*
CYL   Communist Youth League
JMJP   *Jen-min Jih-pao*
NCNA   New China News Agency
NDYL   New Democratic Youth League
SCMM   *Selections from China Mainland Magazines*
SCMP   *Survey of China Mainland Press*

I
Introduction

Youth have been at the forefront of political action in China for half a century. They contributed heavily, both intellectually and physically, to political struggles in republican China. The great movements of May Fourth, December Ninth, and to a lesser extent May Thirtieth, were dominated in certain phases by students, while political organizations generally drew much of their manpower from the ranks of youth. Both the Kuomintang and the Chinese Communist Party [CCP] recognized the importance of this segment of the population by establishing auxiliary youth organizations to mobilize young people in support of their respective goals. Since the establishment of the Chinese People's Republic in 1949, youth have assumed an even more prominent role. They have not only continued to throw themselves into irregular political upheavals, of which the Great Proletarian Cultural Revolution is the best and most recent example, but they have also been more fully utilized than ever before as the regular shock troops of a revolutionary movement because of their relatively great separation from traditional influences.

The purpose of this paper is not to describe or analyze fully the youth movement in Communist China, important though that task is.[1] Our objective is the more modest one of gaining some insights into this critical area of Chinese political life by examining in detail a particular part of it. The subject selected for special attention is *Chung-kuo Ch'ing-nien* (Chinese Youth), the official semi-monthly magazine of the Central Committee of the Communist Youth League. As an official organ of the CCP's youth auxiliary, *Chung-kuo Ch'ing-nien* is by definition one of the more prominent publications in China. Its value as one means of studying Chinese politics may be introduced more meaningfully, however, by a

---

[1] Despite general recognition of the significance of youth movements in modern China, few sustained studies of the subject have been published in English. Important analyses of the pre-Communist period can be found in Chow Tse-tsung, *The May Fourth Movement: Intellectual Revolution in Modern China* (Cambridge, Mass., 1960); John Israel, *Student Nationalism in China, 1927–1937* (Stanford, 1966); and Kiang Wen-han, *The Chinese Student Movement* (New York, 1948). Published material on the Communist youth movement is scarcer, but see Klaus H. Pringsheim, "The Functions of the Chinese Communist Youth Leagues (1920–1949)," *China Quarterly*, No. 12 (October–December 1962); E. Stuart Kirby, ed., *Youth in China* (Hong Kong, 1965); and "What Has Happened to the Youth Corps," *China News Analysis* [hereafter *CNA*], Nos. 633 and 634 (October 21 and 28, 1966).

few general comments on the role of youth and the communications media in Communist China.

Several considerations account for the special emphasis and concern that characterize Party policy toward Chinese youth. There is first of all the historical fact that youth in modern China have been among the most willing and committed recruits to movements aimed at significant social change. In a society in whch traditional values have furnished powerful support for resistance to change, the willingness of youth to question and reject the standards of their elders has been an unmistakable opportunity for revolutionary elites. To this opportunity, the Communist leaders have responded quickly and vigorously. They have played openly on the impatience and idealism of young people, encouraged them in their revolt against tradition, and, most importantly, given them meaningful roles, albeit mainly at lower levels of organization, in carrying out the Party's program. Explicit acknowledgment of the Party's reliance on youth permeates CCP doctrine.[2]

Second, in common with most countries in early stages of industrialization, China has a relatively young population. Although no precise figures are available, in 1965 somewhere between 56.7 and 59.3 per cent of the population was under 25 years of age.[3] In giving great attention to the indoctrination, utilization, and recruitment of youth, the Chinese Communists are, in a sense, simply responding to the political implications of China's demography.

Finally, Chinese Communist leadership has become increasingly concerned about how today's youth will perform as they rise to positions of responsibility in the future. No doubt every elite is sensitive to the question of succession, seeking some way of guaranteeing the prolongation of the policies for which it has struggled. The Chinese leaders are exceptionally sensitive to this problem, however, partly because of their advanced age as a group and partly because of their obsessive fear that China may slide into "revisionist" ways. The reasons for this obsession, and the extent to which it motivates different sections of the leadership, are complex and debatable questions which cannot be considered here, although we shall examine some aspects of the problem in more detail later. The important point is that the CCP regards the fulfillment of the revolutionary potential of Chinese youth not only as an opportunity but as a political imperative. To the extent that this potential is realized, youth form one of the great bulwarks of the revolution; but to the extent that it

---

[2] See, for example, the statements about youth in Mao Tse-tung's famous "red book," *Quotations from Chairman Mao Tse-tung* (Peking, 1966), pp. 288–293. Although the quotations reflect the Party's more recent concern about loss of revolutionary fervor among youth, it is significant that some of Mao's earlier tributes to the inherent progressiveness of youth are also included.

[3] John S. Aird, "Population Growth and Distribution in Mainland China," *An Economic Profile of Mainland China* (Washington, D.C., 1967), vol. II, p. 365.

is not realized, they constitute a threat to the future of the revolution. It is this orientation toward the uncertainties of the future that gives CCP youth policy its urgency and infuses it with such insistent demands that Chinese youth revolutionize themselves. As the word "revolutionize" implies, the present Chinese leadership seeks a personal transformation in every young person, a transformation that will lead youth beyond support for the Party's current policies and on to a permanent inner commitment to "revolutionary" behavior and goals.

In this struggle to revolutionize Chinese youth, the communications media play a critical and revealing role. The growth of a modern communications network is intimately connected to more general processes of social change; it may be regarded, in the modern world, as a necessary condition for the progressive spread of a national political culture and for increased interaction between state and citizen.[4] Communist China is no exception. Although the CCP developed with relatively little reliance on modern means of communication, due to the low cultural level of the population with which it was in contact and the obvious limitations of a guerrilla movement, it wasted no time after its seizure of power in utilizing and expanding the communications structure then existing in China.[5] Despite the Party's continued reliance on, and perhaps preference for, informal communications of the face-to-face variety, the formal communications media are an indispensable part of the Chinese political process.[6]

We are concerned in this study of *Chung-kuo Ch'ing-nien* with one type of formal communications media—the mass media. The mass media in China differ significantly, of course, from their counterparts in democratic systems. They place little priority on the "impartial" dissemination of news, or on the expression of public opinion and official response to it; they may perform these functions to some extent but their chief duties lie elsewhere. The specific function that identifies the Chinese mass media, and distinguishes them from other Chinese communications media, with which they share total subordination to Party objectives, is to disseminate as widely as possible the message or material which the Party wants the masses to receive. The masses do not necessarily receive this message directly, although the readership and circulation of the mass media are relatively large by Chinese standards. The point is that the contents of the mass media are designed for ultimate popular consumption, whether by

---

[4] Lucian W. Pye, ed., *Communications and Political Development* (Princeton, 1963).

[5] For detailed study of communications structure and policy in Communist China, see Franklin Houn, *To Change a Nation: Propaganda and Indoctrination in Communist China* (Glencoe, 1959); and Frederick T. C. Yu, *Mass Persuasion in Communist China* (New York, 1964).

[6] See the discussion in Franz Schurmann, *Ideology and Organization in Communist China* (Berkeley, 1966), pp. 58–68.

direct reading or by transmission to the people through the medium of a basic-level cadre. The latter case may in fact be more common because of low reading skills among much of the population and the desirability of informed explanation of the contents.

The mass media may not appear particularly significant at first glance, since their main function is neither to describe conditions and attitudes at the popular level, nor to provide a complete record and interpretation of official policy. They are, however, a vital link in communications between the central authority and the people, a position which is critically important in the Chinese political system. There are two main reasons why this is so.

The first stems from the demands of political socialization in a society in which there is such an enormous gap between the existing political culture and the ideal political culture desired by political elites. The creation of universal "socialist consciousness" cannot be entrusted to traditional agents of socialization, such as the family, which have been the stronghold of values now destined for elimination. So far as possible, socialization must become a public responsibility, carried out largely through the state-controlled educational system. However, the educational system as such is not equal to the task, even under the best of conditions, simply because it cannot reach the non-school population and cannot control socialization experiences outside the classroom. In effect, therefore, the Communists have committed themselves to the task of "re-schooling" the entire population; without "resocialization" of adults and older youth, even the efforts spent on the youngest generation may be wasted. Herein lies the importance of the mass media, which assume a heavy responsibility for the definition and propagation of the new political culture and which become, in functional terms, part of the educational system.

The second reason for the special importance of the mass media in China is the Party's reliance on popular assistance in the execution of its policies. The Party expects the masses to be informed about current policies and to take concrete action to ensure their implementation. Obviously, the process cannot work without adequate transmittal of information about policy and without some delegation of responsibility for action at specific times and places. Again, the mass media become the link that ensures an adequate flow of communications from top to bottom.

These points are fundamental to an understanding of the mass media in Communist China. It is all too easy to say that these media are dull, repetitious, stifled by political controls, and not exceptionally informative on either top-level policy or popular attitudes. All this is true, at least most of the time. The fact remains that their part in the political education of the people and the CCP's efforts to mobilize the people for action makes them virtually indispensable. It has been observed that communications play an influential role in any political system because the performance of other functions is heavily dependent on their effectiveness.[7] The popular confusion and loss of direction that followed the disruption of communications in China during the Cultural Revolution supports this observation. The Maoists suspended many media simply to deny their use to the opposition, but the uncertainty caused by the loss of these "stereotyped" channels of communication was felt throughout the system.

Our study of *Chung-kuo Ch'ing-nien* is not, therefore, simply a study of propaganda narrowly conceived. It is an avenue for exploring how the regime has managed its links with the young people of China and how it has tried to structure their role in the political process. At the same time, this exploration should also prepare the way for analysis of some of the substantive issues of the youth movement in Communist China.

[7] Gabriel A. Almond and G. Bingham Powell, Jr., *Comparattve Politics: A Developmental Approach* (Boston, 1966), pp. 171–72.

II
Chung-kuo Ch'ing-nien:
Organization and Role

The Chinese Communist Youth League *(Chung-kuo Kung-ch'an-chu-i Ch'ing-nien T'uan)* [CYL] has a history almost as long as its parent organization, the CCP. The Socialist Youth League, which was the Party's first youth auxiliary and which the CYL regards as its founding organization, held its First Congress in May 1922. In 1925, at its Third Congress, it changed its name to Communist Youth League. From 1935 to 1949, as part of its United Front policy designed to attract all anti-Japanese (and later all anti-Kuomintang) youth, the CCP operated without an official Party youth organization; the CYL was replaced by a variety of front organizations under varying degrees of Communist control. The League was re-established in April 1949, by order of the Party Central Committee, under the name of the New Democratic Youth League *(Chung-kuo Hsin Min-chu-chu-i Ch'ing-nien T'uan)* [NDYL]. The NDYL held its Second Congress in June–July 1953 and its Third Congress in May 1957. At the latter congress, the name was again changed to the Communist Youth League. The CYL held its Ninth Congress—the first since the Third Congress of the NDYL, but the ninth counting all previous League congresses—in June 1964.[8] No congress has been held since 1964, and the CYL itself has been inactive since the summer of 1966 as a consequence of the Cultural Revolution.

In the words of its current Constitution, adopted at the Ninth Congress, the CYL is a "school for the study of communism, and an assistant to the CCP;" it does its work "under the leadership of the CCP" and its committees at various levels accept the leadership of Party committees at the same or higher levels.[9] Membership is open to acceptable youth between the ages of 15 and 25, although the Constitution permits cadres to continue working in the League until they are 28. CYL membership was 500,000 in October 1949. It increased to 9 million by June 1953, 23 million by May 1957, and 25 million by May 1959.[10] Since the latter

---

[8] Pringsheim, *op. cit.,* and American Consulate General (Hong Kong), *Current Background* [hereafter *CB*], No. 738 (July 30, 1964). See also "Ch'ing-nien T'uan Li-shih Ts'an-k'ao Tzu-liao" (Reference Materials on the History of the Youth League), *Chung-kuo Ch'ing-nien* [hereafter *CKCN*], Nos. 4–6 (1957).

[9] *CB*, No. 738, pp. 23–24.

[10] Pringsheim, *op. cit.,* pp. 90–91.

14

date, membership has been a chronic and serious problem for the CYL. In January 1962, 25 million was still given as the membership figure.[11] The Ninth Congress in 1964 released no new membership figures, even though membership figures at the convocation of all previous congresses were reported at that time. CYL First Secretary Hu Yao-pang stated at the Ninth Congress that membership had "increased significantly" during the previous two or three years, but he failed to expand on this remark.[12] It is safe to assume that membership remained relatively constant from 1959 up to the launching of a major recruitment campaign in 1965. As later discussion will show, the real problem is not simply one of absolute numbers. With 25 million members drawn from a reported "youth" population of 130 million, nearly 20 per cent of those eligible by age are members—not at all a low figure for an elite organization. It is the quality, age, and social status of League members that has caused concern in recent years.

The history of official youth publications also extends back to the earliest days of the Chinese Communist movement. *Chung-kuo Ch'ing-nien* began publication in Shanghai as the weekly organ of the Socialist Youth League on October 20, 1923, with Yün Tai-ying as Editor-in-Chief. It was suspended in the spring of 1927 by the Kuomintang, but resumed as a secret publication in Shanghai under the name of *Wu-ch'an Ch'ing-nien* (Proletarian Youth) in November 1927. The name was changed to *Lieh-ning Ch'ing-nien* (Leninist Youth) in October 1928, with publication continuing in Shanghai until 1932. From 1932, the magazine was published in Juichin under the title *Ch'ing-nien Shih-hua* (Young Truth), but publication ceased with the start of the Long March in October 1934. During these years, Jen Pi-shih, who was to be a leading figure of the Communist youth movement until his death in 1950, assumed directorship of the magazine. *Chung-kuo Ch'ing-nien* revived as a monthly in Yenan from 1939 to 1942, under the Youth Work Committee of the CCP Central Committee. The present *Chung-kuo Ch'ing-nien* began publication on December 20, 1948, in P'ingshan *Hsien,* Hopei, again under the direction of the Youth Work Committee. After its fourth issue, it moved to its permanent location in Peking. It initially resumed publication as a monthly, became a weekly, and then, in early 1950, became a bi-weekly (26 issues per year); subsequently, it became a semi-monthly (24 issues per year), which it remained down to its suspension in August 1966.[13]

---

[11] *Jen-min Jih-pao* (People's Daily) [hereafter *JMJP*] January 22, 1962, cited in *CNA,* No. 633.

[12] *CB,* No. 738, pp. 18–19.

[13] "Chieh-shao 'Chung-kuo Ch'ing-nien'" (Introducing "Chinese Youth"), *CK CN,* No. 50 (October 21, 1950); and "'Chung-kuo Ch'ing-nien' Ssu-shih Nien ti Kai-k'uang" (General Conditions of "Chinese Youth's" Forty Years), *Chung-kuo Ch'ing-nien Pao* (Chinese Youth Journal) [hereafter cited as *CKCNP*], October 19, 1963.

Since the Chinese Communists release very little information on the internal organization and staffing of their publications, it is possible to construct only a general picture of the organization of *Chung-kuo Ch'ing-nien.*[14] The magazine is published and distributed by the Chinese Youth Press *(Chung-kuo Ch'ing-nien Ch'u-pan-she),* which was established in 1950 as the publishing agent of the Central Committee of the Youth League.[15] Formal statements always identify *Chung-kuo Ch'ing-nien* as "the official magazine of the Youth League's Central Committee." However, although it is clear that the League's Central Committee is formally responsible for the publication of the magazine, there are two other agencies which exercise some control over it. One of these is the Ministry of Culture's Bureau of Publications, which administers state regulations pertaining to printing and publishing enterprises. In the early years of the regime, such administrative controls were an important part of the Party's effort to bring the existing publications industry into its propaganda network. Regulations gave state publications offices sweeping powers to approve present and future publishing activities; to require full information on staff, facilities, scope of operations and plans before granting permission to operate; and to ensure that all publications observed certain political standards and restrictions in their contents.[16] After the first few years, however, these regulations simply described the accomplished fact of Party control. The Bureau of Publications provides a formal administrative channel for enforcing CCP decisions concerning publications, but it is unlikely that it has any significant influence over an organ such as *Chung-kuo Ch'ing-nien.*

The other, and more important, line of control is through the Propaganda Department of the CCP Central Committee. The Propaganda Department, headed by Lu Ting-yi until his removal in the spring of 1966,

---

[14] Much of the following discussion is based on information obtained from Chinese refugees. Although, as mentioned above, *Chung-kuo Ch'ing-nien* suspended publication in August 1966, the following discussion is framed, for convenience, in the present tense.

[15] Feng Wen-pin, "Chung-kuo Hsin Min-chu-chu-i Ch'ing-nien T'uan Shih Chung-kuo Ch'ing-nien Ko-ming Tou-cheng Ch'uan-t'ung ti Chi-ch'eng-che" (The NDYL Is the Heir to Chinese Youth's Tradition of Revolutionary Struggle), *CK CN*, No. 63 (April 21, 1951).

[16] See "Cheng-wu-yüan Kuan-yü Kai-chin ho Fa-chan Ch'üan-kuo Ch'u-pan Shih-yeh ti Chih-shih" (Directive of the Government Administrative Council on Advancing and Developing National Publications Work), *Hsin-hua Yüeh-pao* (New China Monthly), No. 13 (November 25, 1950); "Kuan-li Shu-k'an Ch'u-pan-yeh Yin-shua-yeh Fa-hsing-yeh Chan-hsing T'iao-li" (Temporary Regulations for Managing the Publishing, Printing and Distribution of Books and Periodicals), *JMJP*, August 19, 1952; and "Ch'i-k'an Teng-chi Chan-shih Pan-fa" (Temporary Methods for the Registration of Periodicals), *JMJP*, August 19, 1952. See also the discussion of controls over publications in Houn, *op. cit.*, pp. 107–116.

exercises general supervision and control over the entire propaganda network throughout the country.[17] Although command relationships in such areas are difficult to distinguish, there is no doubt that this department sets basic policy for a journal like *Chung-kuo Ch'ing-nien* and approves key appointments to its staff. Since Lu Ting-yi was also Minister of Culture, and since the CCP regards the cultural and educational ministries as part of the same governmental sub-system of propaganda affairs, state administrative controls over publications do not hamper the Propaganda Department's authority in these matters. In the case of *Chung-kuo Ch'ing-nien,* conflicts of authority would more likely arise between the Party Propaganda Department and the CYL Central Committee. Even here, however, the Propaganda Department is technically supreme, since the League's supervision of the magazine is probably entrusted to its own Propaganda Department, which is in turn subordinate to the Party's Propaganda Department.

The suspension of *Chung-kuo Ch'ing-nien* and *Chung-kuo Ch'ing-nien Pao* (Chinese Youth Journal), the official newspaper of the CYL Central Committee, in August 1966 suggests that purges at the top levels of League publications have occurred, or will occur before these organs resume publication. As of May 1967, however, no purges had been announced. Although it is not possible to compile a complete list of key staff members, Table I gives the names of some individuals identified with League publications up to 1966. Some of these people have contributed articles to the publications in question which should aid in understanding any purges made public in the future.

The operation of *Chung-kuo Ch'ing-nien* rests on three informal personnel groupings: editors, reporters and correspondents. The editorial staff includes the Director *(She-chang),* the Editor-in-Chief *(Tsung pien-chi),* a few Deputy Editors-in-Chief *(Fu-tsung pien-chi)* and an uncertain number of other editors; in all they may number about fifteen. The editorial staff monopolizes decisions and responsibility. Appointed, or at least approved, by the CCP Propaganda Department, they are cadres experienced in the propaganda system and somewhat advanced in the League or Party hierarchy. Their decisions on publication policy are informed and guided by direct instructions on the current line from the CCP Propaganda Department, buttressed by meetings of League and Party cells within the magazine's staff.

Chung-kuo Ch'ing-nien reporters *(chi-che)* are regular, full-time employees who work mainly in the editorial office in Peking, although they may occasionally be sent to other areas for special investigations and reports. Unlike the editors, they need have little propaganda or journalistic experience and are not necessarily League or Party members. Many

---

[17] See Houn, *op. cit.,* pp. 22–26, and Yu, *op. cit.,* Chap. 4.

TABLE I

KEY STAFF MEMBERS OF CYL PUBLICATIONS

Position	Name	Date mentioned in position	Comments and Other Positions
CKCN			
Deputy Editor-in-Chief	Hsia Yü-ssu	Aug. 1963	
CKCNP			
Director	Sun I-ch'ing	Jan. 1962	NDYL Propaganda Department, Feb. 1956; CKCNP Editor-in-Chief, Dec. 1958; Standing Committee of CYL Central Committee, July 1964.
Editor-in-Chief	Liu Ch'ing-fang	Sept. 1964	CYL Central Committee, July 1964.
Deputy Editor-in-Chief	Hsü Ts'ai	April 1963	CYL Central Committee, July 1964.
Deputy Editor-in-Chief	Wang Shih-ku	Nov. 1965	
Former Director and Editor-in-Chief	Chang Li-ch'ün		In July 1957, criticized his "errors" of May 1957.
Former Deputy Editor-in-Chief	Ch'en Mo		"Anti-Party activities" exposed in September 1957; membership on CYL Central Committee revoked in January 1958.
China Youth Press			
Director	Pien Ch'un-kuang	Jan. 1961	Standing Committee of CYL Central Committee, July 1964.
CYL Propaganda Department			
Deputy Director	Huang T'ien-hsiang	Aug. 1961	Standing Committee of CYL Central Committee, March 1960; not elected to CYL Central Committee at Ninth Congress in July 1964; published article in *CKCN* on Feb. 16, 1964.
Deputy Director	Lu Ching	Sept. 1960	
Former Director	Yang Hai-po		First reported as Director of Propaganda Department, Oct. 1957; elected Secretary of CYL Central Committee, March 1960; reelected, July 1964; presumably left Propaganda Department for higher position.

are young college graduates, assigned to *Chung-kuo Ch'ing-nien* at least partly because of their relatively high academic preparation and literary skill. Political activism is, of course, a consideration, but it is not crucial at this level. The job is an attractive one because of the urban location, the type of work, and the opportunities for rewarding experiences and contacts; reporters are not likely to risk the loss of such a position by withholding the necessary activism. In any case, a reporter's work is supervised too closely, both by the editors and by political "study" groups among the staff, to allow much opportunity for political deviation. In October 1950, the magazine had 59 "special reporters" *(t'e-yüeh chi-che)*;[18] the term connotes a less regular position than a reporter, but the figure may give a rough clue to the size of the reportorial staff at that time. The staffs of all major Chinese publications, including *Chung-kuo Ch'ing-nien,* were reduced after 1957 as a result of the "anti-rightist" campaign of that year and the practice of sending cadres down to work at lower levels *(hsia-fang).* The total number of regular employees of *Chung-kuo Ch'ing-nien* in recent years is a mystery, although it is probably somewhere between fifty and one hundred.

Correspondents *(t'ung-hsün-yüan)* and "special correspondents" *(t'e-yüeh t'ung-hsün-yüan),* who constitute the third category, are not part of the regular staff of *Chung-kuo Ch'ing-nien.* They are people scattered about the country who have agreed to assist the editors on an irregular basis by supplying copy, reflecting local opinions, soliciting and writing letters-to-the-editor, and encouraging the reading of the magazine. The great majority are no doubt students or CYL members and cadres. There were 670 of them in October 1950, and efforts were then in progress to enlarge their numbers.[19] Though irregular, the work they do is important, since the editors rely on them for a volume and variety of material which the regular reporters in Peking cannot match.

Internal organization of the magazine follows obvious lines. Business functions are separate from editorial functions; the latter are handled by several sections covering such subjects as daily assignments, political affairs, economic affairs, cultural and educational affairs, League affairs, and letters from readers. The letters section, which is part of all mainland publications, deserves special mention. Its function is to read and file all letters received and to respond to them either by direct answer or by referral to the agency most appropriate for the question or problem raised; in the case of referral, the section may ensure a response by follow-up checks with the office in question. The mass media in particular take this duty very seriously, since it is one aspect of the CCP's "mass line" and is backed up by directives specifying procedures for satisfactory responses

---

[18] "Introducing 'Chinese Youth,' " *op. cit.*
[19] *Ibid.*

to all letters received.[20] The practice underscores the fact that *Chung-kuo Ch'ing-nien* and the other mass media are not merely propaganda outlets but are, instead, two-way communications links. Most of the communication may be downward, but there is at least some opportunity for upward communications and response. By soliciting letters, and devoting special care to their handling, *Chung-kuo Ch'ing-nien* gets some sense of what its readers are thinking about, and makes some effort to engage in dialogue with them.

The letters section is not in charge of the "letters from readers" column that appears in the magazine. The publication of letters, and the choice of what public response to make, is a more sensitive matter that calls for decision from higher editorial levels. The letters section will, of course, bring certain letters to the attention of the editors, and it may recommend publication or be ordered to draft a response. Nevertheless, it is the editors who decide what to print, and their decision will rest primarily on current propaganda priorities. Thus, the letters that appear in *Chung-kuo Ch'ing-nien* are a small and probably unrepresentative sample of all letters received. Since their publication stems from propaganda considerations, certain types of letters may be solicited at certain times, or even be ghosted by a staff member, in order to provoke a desired debate or discussion in the pages of the magazine. No doubt most published letters are genuine, however, in the sense that they come from someone not on the staff who has a real personal problem or a question to raise. The point is that such letters are not necessarily a good sample of readers' opinions, nor is their publication necessarily based on the merits or importance of the question raised. The contents of *all* letters received would be much more revealing, but that is information reserved for the editorial staff and higher authorities, not for the readers of *Chung-kuo Ch'ing-nien*.

The solicitation of both letters and articles from non-staff members is not simply a result of editorial demand for copy. To be sure, the editors benefit from a large and varied flow of contributions from which to select the magazine's contents. There is no evidence, however, that *Chung-kuo Ch'ing-nien* is significantly short of copy, even though it stresses regularly the importance of receiving materials from its readers.[21] The explanation, again, lies in the Party's insistence that the mass media be more than one-way propaganda channels. Specifically, they have organizational responsibilities which include both the activation of local units and the upward and outward transmission of local information. In April 1949,

---

[20] James R. Townsend, *Political Participation in Communist China* (Berkeley, 1967), pp. 177–78.

[21] In 1950, *CKCN*'s editors reported that they received an average of about 700 articles and letters every month; "Introducing 'Chinese Youth,'" *op. cit.* The magazine would probably not use much more than one-tenth of these in a month (two issues).

Feng Wen-pin, then a Secretary of the NDYL Central Committee, made this point clear in his report to the NDYL's First Congress:

> League committees at various levels ought to give full attention to this publication [*Chung-kuo Ch'ing-nien*], mobilizing League members and youth generally to submit articles to it, offering opinions to it, organizing its reporting and promoting its publication. They must make this publication perform an organizational function as well as its propaganda and educational function.[22]

The implementation of this principle has been a continuing concern of the League Central Committee. In a directive of August 3, 1950, it stated that all League committees must strengthen their reporting to *Chung-kuo Ch'ing-nien* and other important communications media in order to expand League propaganda and the communication of youth work experience; it instructed League committees at provincial and municipal levels to produce at least one report or article every three months on the solution of practical youth problems.[23] The directive establishing *Chung-kuo Ch'ing-nien Pao* was even more explicit on this point. Stating that NDYL committee members must submit copy and opinions to the new newspaper and urge the members of their units to do the same, it ordered the designation of special reporters for *Chung-kuo Ch'ing-nien Pao* within League committee propaganda departments so as to fix responsibility for the submission of material and for the completion of any tasks the editors might assign. It also stated that League secretaries should check to make sure that every member of the Central Committee wrote at least one article per year for the newspaper, and that every member of regional and provincial committees wrote at least one article every six months.[24] This theme received further emphasis in a directive of November 16, 1957, which insisted that the submission of materials to League publications was a regular responsibility of CYL cadres; to this end, the chiefs or deputy chiefs of the propaganda departments in all League committees were to organize reporters' small groups to ensure a regular flow of articles, letters, opinions, demands and information about youth work and problems to these publications.[25] Ideally, therefore, *Chung-kuo Ch'ing-*

---

[22] Feng Wen-pin, "Chung-kuo Hsin Min-chu-chu-i Ch'ing-nien T'uan ti Jen-wu yü Kung-tso" (The Tasks and Work of the NDYL), in *Chung-kuo Hsin Min-chu-chu-i Ch'ing-nien T'uan ti Jen-wu yü Kung-tso* (Shanghai, 1949).

[23] NDYL Central Committee, "Kuan-yü Chia-ch'iang T'uan ti Hsüan-ch'uan Chiao-yü Kung-tso ti Chüeh-ting" (Decision on Strengthening League Propaganda and Educational Work), *CKCN*, No. 45 (August 12, 1950).

[24] NDYL Central Committee, "Kuan-yü Ch'u-pan 'Chung-kuo Ch'ing-nien Pao' ti Chüeh-ting" (Decision on the Publication of *CKCNP*), *Hsin-hua Yüeh-pao*, No. 15 (May 25, 1951).

[25] CYL Central Committee, "Kuan-yü Chia-ch'iang T'uan-pao T'uan-k'an ti T'ung-hsün, Yüeh-tu, Fa-hsing Kung-tso ti Chih-shih" (Directive on Strengthening Reporting, Reading and Distribution Work of League Newspapers and Periodicals), *CKCN*, No. 23 (December 1, 1957).

nien and other publications of its type are vehicles for increasing the organizational activity and interest of the members of the organizations they serve and for disseminating information about organizational life. How well *Chung-kuo Ch'ing-nien* accomplishes these objectives is difficult to judge, since much of the communication that it so deliberately promotes is never published in the magazine. The explicitness of the recurrent directives, however, suggests there may be room for improvement.

CIRCULATION AND READERSHIP

Table II reveals some of the fluctuations in the circulation of *Chung-kuo Ch'ing-nien*. The period of greatest growth was from July 1953 to March 1956, probably reflecting the relative stability and "normalization" that followed the armistice in Korea. Although March 1956 apparently stands

TABLE II
CIRCULATION OF *CHUNG-KUO CH'ING-NIEN*

Date	Circulation
October 1950[a]	130,000
June 1953[b]	390,000
December 1953[b]	670,000
March 1954[b]	910,000
April 1954[b]	1,090,000
January 1956[c]	1,664,555
March 1956[c]	1,849,021
January 1957[c]	1,558,382
June 1957[c]	1,783,991
January 1958[c]	1,071,405
June 1958[c]	1,299,532
September 1958[c]	1,237,767
October 1963[d]	1,450,000

Sources:
[a] "Introducing 'Chinese Youth,' " *CKCN*, No. 50 (October 21, 1950).
[b] *Ta Kung Pao* (Hong Kong), July 11, 1954.
[c] *CKCN*, number of copies printed given in magazine.
[d] *CKCNP*, October 19, 1963.

as the magazine's peak, circulation remained high until June 1957. The rapid decline during the last six month of 1957 was almost certainly a consequence of the Anti-Rightist campaign that began in June of that year and uncovered many "errors" in both publication and youth work. Circulation increased slightly in early 1958 but began to decline at the middle of the year. With Number 18 (September 16) of 1958, *Chung-kuo Ch'ing-nien* stopped releasing in each issue the number of copies printed, a practice it had observed since 1956. Shortages of newsprint and possible difficulties in distribution presumably account for the decline in circulation and the consequent decision to withhold circulation figures; decline in the volume of mainland publications was a general phenomenon during the Great Leap Forward. By 1963, circulation was partially restored but still substantially below the 1956 peak.

Although these circulation figures do not appear large relative to the population, the magazine is one of the most widely distributed journals in China. In 1954, it had the largest circulation of all Chinese periodicals,[26] and it is always described as one of the largest circulation magazines. Its relative importance is more evident when one looks at the total circulation of magazines in China. This total figure was 900,000 in 1951 and 17 million in 1958;[27] *Chung-kuo Ch'ing-nien* thus accounted for perhaps 20 per cent of the total in 1951 and about 7 per cent in 1958.

Its large circulation relative to other mainland publications notwithstanding, *Chung-kuo Ch'ing-nien* has plainly been dissatisfied since 1957 with the size of its reading public. The problem is partly one of absolute circulation figures and partly one of arrangements for group use of single copies. Circulation figures are one measure of readership, but a more critical question may be how many people read each copy. Most subscriptions come from libraries, reading rooms and League branches, with the understanding that cadres and other individuals will see to it that the potential audience actually reads the magazine or has its contents made known to them.

Although the League has emphasized this matter from the first, the reexamination of youth work that followed the Hundred Flowers campaign of 1957 brought open criticism. In November 1957, the CYL Central Committee announced that "recent investigations" had shown that some literate League members and cadres had not been reading the official League organs, had read them infrequently, or were not emphasizing sufficiently their use in study. It was essential, the Central Committee said, for League branches to strengthen their organized reading and study of these publications; they must work with local post offices to improve distribution, provide League funds for unit subscriptions and also encourage individual subscriptions.[28] Following this directive, a drive for a "leap forward" in the reading of League publications ensued. It was pointed out in discussions that, despite improvements during the Anti-Rightist campaign, reading of League materials was not sufficiently systematic. For example, too few units or individuals held subscriptions to *Chung-kuo Ch'ing-nien* and *Chung-kuo Ch'ing-nien Pao*; in some cases, League branches subscribed to the newspaper but made individuals pay for their own subscriptions to the magazine, with the natural result that there were few subscriptions to the latter; and too many units or libraries subscribed to only one copy when there was sufficient demand to justify extra copies.[29]

---

[26] *Ta Kung Pao* (Hong Kong), July 11, 1954.

[27] *JMJP*, editorial, March 16, 1958, cited in Yu, *op. cit.*, p. 90.

[28] "Directive on Strengthening Reporting, Reading and Distribution Work of League Newspapers and Periodicals," *op. cit.*

[29] See the articles in *CKCN*, No. 6 (March 16, 1958).

Circulation figures show that *Chung-kuo Ch'ing-nien*'s "leap forward" was a failure, probably for reasons beyond the editors' or the League's control. In addition to newsprint shortages, the disruptions of the Great Leap period, particularly the practice of *hsia-fang,* were formidable obstacles to the campaign to increase readership. The November 1957 directive cited above acknowledged that the transfer of League cadres and other youth to the countryside affected readership adversely because League publications were not well distributed in the villages. Changes of residence no doubt caused delay or loss of individual subscriptions, too. The magazine's basic problems and the dissatisfaction over them that appeared at this time were apparently never overcome, for, as we shall note later, *Chung-kuo Ch'ing-nien* was to launch another effort to increase its readership in 1965.

DEFINITION OF ROLE

The preceding discussion of some of *Chung-kuo Ch'ing-nien*'s organizational problems has opened up a number of issues relating to the magazine's role in Chinese politics. These issues divide into two general categories: the definition of its role and its internal political problems. Problems of role definition include uncertainty about the magazine's place in the Chinese communications system and difficulties in fulfilling its assigned tasks. Political problems refer to the existence within the magazine of opposition to the Party's line or authority.

Conflict arising from definition of role is not necessarily serious or disruptive. The evidence indicates that *Chung-kuo Ch'ing-nien*'s problems in this area have been neither exceptionally severe nor inherently unmanageable. However, Communist China is a highly organized society in which the leadership accepts the idea of division of labor and usually makes very explicit statements about the roles, functions and responsibilities of different organizations. In reality, of course, such distinctions may break down or become obscure—the CCP itself is perhaps the most flagrant offender against formal delineations of organizational authority. But it is also true that Party organizations, or at least individual Party cadres, are frequently criticized for exceeding or failing to fulfill their formal roles. For subordinate organizations, such violations become constant invitations to criticism and interference from the outside. An organization which experiences confusion or difficulty in carrying out its duties can thus have little sense of confidence or autonomy. To some extent, this appears to have happened to *Chung-kuo Ch'ing-nien*.

In formal terms, the magazine has at least three roles, each associated with different functions and a different focus in contents. First, it is a Party propaganda organ, designed to present and explain the Party line to the youth of China and to secure both their behavioral and ideological support for this line. This role leads to a pronounced emphasis on theoretical argumentation, exposition of general policy, and heavy-handed exhortation to reform one's thought and work. Second, it is a "house organ" of the Youth League, with the function of assisting and improving the League's organizational life. The emphasis here is on reproduction and discussion of documents specific to the youth movement; on providing materials, such as biographies of "models" and "heroes" or reports on basic-level League units, which give concrete descriptions of approved behavior and organization; and on soliciting comment and promoting discussion on a wide range of organizational policies, such as admission, study time, procedure in meetings, personal conflicts and so forth. This role calls for a simple, down-to-earth style, since it aims at a broad and in many cases not highly literate readership. Finally, *Chung-kuo Ch'ing-nien* is a magazine for Chinese youth generally, although this is naturally understood to mean "progressive" youth who are basically sympathetic to the Communist cause. As such, it provides a medium for general education, expression, and even entertainment for young people—again, of course, with the understanding that nothing contrary to the official line will be tolerated. This role naturally suggests a more literate readership, mainly students, and a more sophisticated approach. General information on China and other countries, articles on modern science and education, relatively open discussion of youth (not simply League) problems, and a relatively large offering of art and literature are the contents representative of the general youth magazine.

These are analytical distinctions, of course, which cannot be applied systematically to the entire contents of the magazine. In practice, *Chung-kuo Ch'ing-nien* can and does achieve some integration of its roles—articles of general interest and literary offerings will still contain a propaganda message, theoretical lessons will be drawn from concrete descriptions, and so forth. The distinctions are useful, however, because official statements not only recognize them as generally valid but also reveal that the magazine has not attained a wholly satisfactory balance among them.

As noted earlier, the CCP has never identified clearly the final source of control over *Chung-kuo Ch'ing-nien*. The magazine began publication in December 1948, when the NDYL was not yet formed, under the Youth Work Committee of the Party Central Committee. When the Central Committee made its January 1949 decision to establish the NDYL, it indicated that *Chung-kuo Ch'ing-nien* would serve youth work but was still a publication of the Youth Work Committee; the failure to identify the magazine as a League publication seems significant in light of the decision's explicit recognition of the "organizational independence" of the NDYL in other areas.[30] Three months later, at the NDYL's First Con-

---

[30] CCP Central Committee, "Kuan-yü Chien-li Chung-kuo Hsin Min-chu-chu-i Ch'ing-nien T'uan ti Chieh-i" (Resolution on Establishing the NDYL), in *Chung-kuo Hsin Min-chu-chu-i Ch'ing-nien T'uan ti Jen-wu yü Kung-tso*.

gress, Feng Wen-pin made the same distinction by stating: "After a short period, the Central Committee of the League will publish its own newspaper. At present, it uses *Chung-kuo Ch'ing-nien,* which is published by the Youth Work Committee of the Party Central Committee, as its official publication." [31] Eighteen months later, the magazine was said to be an "official publication of the NDYL Central Committee," a phrase which thereafter became the standard identification; the relationship to the Party Central Committee remained obscure, however, as the same statement noted that the magazine had begun publication under the Youth Work Committee and had subsequently been "designated" as the official organ of the Youth League.[32] The point, of course, is not that *Chung-kuo Ch'ing-nien* has no ultimate controlling agency; it is rather that it serves two different organizations, which unavoidably enlarges and complicates its role.

More direct statements about *Chung-kuo Ch'ing-nien*'s duties confirm this impression. The CCP Central Committee resolution on establishing the NDYL used a brief phrase which became the standard description of the magazine's functions and which also tersely recognized the combination of organizational and propaganda roles; the magazine was "to guide Youth League work throughout the country and to organize youth for study." [33] The third role of a general youth magazine was also implicit in the resolution's directions that the NDYL unite and educate the "broad masses" of youth. The resolution called on the League "to study cultural, scientific, production and military knowledge, to study professions and techniques, and to enable every League member to raise himself ideologically, politically, culturally and in his work." League publications would obviously assume much of the responsibility for implementing this order. Feng Wen-pin, speaking for the League, echoed all of these points and also commented that the League "must systematically educate League members and the masses of youth outside the League in Marxism-Leninism and the thought of Mao Tse-tung, and must use this publication [*Chung-kuo Ch'ing-nien*] to enable them to solve those problems which most closely concern them." In subsequent comments, however, Feng chose to emphasize particularly the magazine's organizational role.[34]

One of the most concrete and empirically accurate descriptions of the magazine's general character occurs in an article which asserts:

> *Chung-kuo Ch'ing-nien* aims at a youth readership of middle cultural level and above, including those workers, peasant cadres, middle school students from the third year on, university students,

[31] Feng Wen-pin, "The Tasks and Work of the NDYL," *op. cit.*
[32] "Introducing 'Chinese Youth,' " *op. cit.*
[33] "Resolution on Establishing the NDYL," *op. cit.*
[34] Feng Wen-pin, "The Tasks and Work of the NDYL," *op. cit.* See also the discussion to which note 22, above, refers.

revolutionary cadres, officials, shopworkers, teachers, etc., who have a middle cultural level.[35]

The key phrases are the references to youth of a "middle cultural level and above," and the more exact "middle school students from the third year on," for these limitations probably exclude a high proportion of workers and perhaps many cadres as well. It should also be noted that non-cadre peasants are not included and that there is no suggestion that the readership consists mainly of League members. The article continues with a description of typical contents, illustrating the magazine's efforts to integrate its multiple roles. Each issue is to have as its core a current, practical problem of thought or work. In addition, each issue will have some materials in the following four categories: 1) editorials and forums—"occasional" editorials, plus three or four "commentaries" per issue on problems that arise in ordinary youth work; 2) the youth movement—"practical and lively" biographies to guide League work and to introduce models, articles for guidance on current movements, articles on League experience in different areas and on intra-League life, materials on the Soviet youth league, and questions and answers on the history of the Chinese and international youth movements; 3) study and self-cultivation—articles to assist youth in study and self-cultivation, which may frequently revolve around a central article and occupy a large number of issues, and which may use the "problem discussion" format to encourage reader participation; 4) literature and art—frequent publication of short stories, biographies of famous people, book reviews, songs and poems, plays, literary guidance, photographs, and so forth.

Chung-kuo Ch'ing-nien has made some efforts to follow this outline, as a glance at the contents of any issue will show, but a further complication of its role emerged with the establishment of *Chung-kuo Ch'ing-nien Pao* in April 1951 and the consequent need to define its division of labor vis-à-vis the latter publication. *Chung-kuo Ch'ing-nien Pao* was told, in effect, to move into literally every field and subject previously assigned to the magazine. The only significant distinction was that the newspaper was to give more systematic attention to documentation of League affairs and was to be "sufficiently simple for both higher and lower cultural level readers to understand." [36] At the same time, the NDYL Central Committee suggested that conflict between the two publications was to be avoided by moving the magazine toward a more specialized role. *Chung-kuo Ch'ing-nien's* "main readers" were to be "youth and youth cadres of a middle cultural level," while its contents would "emphasize the theory and analysis, through Marxism-Leninism and the thought of Mao Tse-tung, of various ideological problems among youth." [37]

---

[35] "Introducing 'Chinese Youth,' " *op. cit.*
[36] "Decision on the Publication of *CKCNP*," *op. cit.*
[37] *Ibid.*

In practice, a rough division along these lines did take place. The newspaper became the main organ of the League Central Committee, while the magazine oriented itself more toward problems of theory and study. But in principle this change was never really accepted. In a very revealing and somewhat defensive statement, shortly after the newspaper began publication, *Chung-kuo Ch'ing-nien*'s editorial staff took up this entire question.[38] First, it announced that it had discovered, by soliciting readers' comments, that its main shortcoming was in its theoretical articles, which were "too many, too long, too dry" and too difficult for many readers to understand. In the future, the editors promised, the magazine would publish more articles of the sort suggested by readers, that is, biographies of heroes and models and discussions of concrete problems. Next, the editors declared "we must make a definite division of labor with the League newspaper." *Chung-kuo Ch'ing-nien Pao* would provide "more direction of current practical work" and "to a greater extent will reflect and solve urgent problems of a timely nature"; its articles would be shorter and fewer, with more pictures, thus creating a journal which would be easier for those of a relatively low cultural level to read. The magazine would aim at youth of a middle cultural level and would "give more emphasis to discussion of problems in youth's thought, study and life."

The problem for the magazine, obviously, was how to do this without magnifying the defect of excessive theorizing and possibly alienating its readership. The editors responded by obscuring much of the "division of labor" which they had just pronounced. In aiming at a "middle cultural level," the magazine had to reflect the "real conditions" of this level; thus, it had to supplement its theoretical approach with concrete examples and stories, and had to carry articles on heroes and models, revolutionary history and League work and problems. Finally, the editors acknowledged many complaints that they were accumulating copy which they were too slow in publishing. This was true, they said, and it was due to the fact that many of their cadres had been taken away with the establishment of the newspaper and that they were now forced to share some of their reporters and correspondents. The creation of the newspaper was plainly a difficult and possibly bitter experience for *Chung-kuo Ch'ing-nien.*

An authoritative assessment of *Chung-kuo Ch'ing-nien*'s performance more than two years later revealed that the same basic dilemma persisted.[39] The assessment praised the magazine as a powerful assistant to the Party in educating youth, citing as its most important feature its ability to link up central Party tasks with the propagandization and education of youth. However, it criticized the magazine for too few articles providing

---

[38] *CKCN,* No. 64 (May 7, 1951), p. 2.

[39] Chang Wei, "Chi-nien 'Chung-kuo Ch'ing-nien' Ch'uang-k'an San-shih Chou-nien" (Commemorate "Chinese Youth's" Thirtieth Anniversary), *JMJP,* October 22, 1953.

guidance for League work and general youth participation in economic construction and for too many "dry and abstract" articles. Basically, this situation remained unchanged down to *Chung-kuo Ch'ing-nien*'s suspension in 1966. On the one hand, the magazine has been popularly regarded as a journal for theoretical study and indoctrination, a role which it has filled reasonably well. On the other hand, in both criticism and self-criticism, it has been attacked as too dry, too theoretical, and too little concerned with day-to-day problems of League organization and youth life in general.

Chung-kuo Ch'ing-nien and *Chung-kuo Ch'ing-nien Pao* are not the only regular League publications; there are a large number of intra-League publications for cadres, some of them secret and authoritative bulletins, as well as many other newspapers and magazines published by League organizations at different levels. There are, however, only the two important central-level publications designed for popular consumption and nationwide distribution, and it is perhaps inevitable that there has been some competition between them. The newspaper has plainly captured the top position in this competition. Apart from the impressions of former mainland residents, who identify the newspaper as the more important of the two, there is ample circumstantial evidence to confirm their relative status. A glance at Table I suggests that the higher cadres of the newspaper must be more prominent and high placed than those of the magazine. It should also be recalled that some League units have provided League funds for purchase of the newspaper but not the magazine. In July 1966, just prior to suspension, *Chung-kuo Ch'ing-nien Pao* appeared much more confident, or at least more willing to fight, than *Chung-kuo Ch'ing-nien*. While the magazine disappeared with scarcely a ripple, the newspaper announced it would not only continue but would step up its publication from three times a week to six times a week.[40] No doubt the main reason for this difference in visibility and viability is the simple fact of frequency of publication. Although both the newspaper and the magazine are held responsible for serving as official organs of the League, it is the newspaper which has all the advantages in prompt and thorough coverage of League affairs. It may be, too, that the League Central Committee has had a preference for the newspaper from the first, since it was established under League auspices whereas the magazine was not.

Chung-kuo Ch'ing-nien's role problems have been largely a product of a closed communications system—a system which sets certain standards for its component parts and which is relatively insensitive to incongru-

---

[40] *CKCNP*, July 25, 1966, in American Consulate General (Hong Kong), *Survey of China Mainland Press* [hereafter cited as *SCMP*], No. 3753 (August 4, 1966). *CKCNP* began publication with two issues per week. On April 1, 1954, it began to publish three times a week (Tuesday, Thursday and Saturday), and on January 1, 1956, stepped up its publication to six times a week (daily except Monday). On January 1, 1962, it reverted to the thrice-weekly schedule.

ities that develop within the prescribed pattern. The magazine's inability to meet fully the standards set for it appear to be due more to this inflexibility and its own lack of autonomy than to inadequacies of staff, technique, or material. In a more open system, the magazine could have altered its role. For example, it could have become more exclusively a general youth magazine or a cadre-oriented theoretical journal. Either of these alternatives would have been plausible in terms of reader demands and Party requirements; some trend toward a theoretical orientation took place even without explicit authorization. However, the CCP and CYL have insisted that *Chung-kuo Ch'ing-nien* continue to fill its several roles, and they have criticized it for falling short of expected performance in any of them.

How can we reconcile this lack of flexibility and responsiveness with earlier comments about Chinese concern for "two-way" communications? The answer is simple yet fundamental, and derives from the pedagogical function which characterizes communications in China. The Chinese Communists approach the task of education with the conviction that basic popular attitudes must be changed. The depth and urgency of this conviction has fluctuated over time, but since 1957 it has been very pronounced. The mass media, which share much of the responsibility for political education, cannot, therefore, be influenced significantly by popular response and demand. They are interested in obtaining this response, for organizational reasons and as a measure of their own effectiveness, but they cannot permit it to dilute the message which the CCP wishes to transmit to the people. Lack of receptiveness to the message is simply taken as evidence of the correctness of the Party's assertion that the political education of the Chinese people is a long-term, arduous struggle. Thus, the leadership's fixed notions about what the mass media ought to accomplish has continued to determine the standards of *Chung-kuo Ching-nien*'s performance despite considerable evidence of built-in frustrations in this role.

POLITICAL PROBLEMS

Before the Cultural Revolution brought on *Chung-kuo Ch'ing-nien*'s suspension and, at least by implication, associated it with political opposition, the magazine had a relatively clean political history. Its pre-1966 problems certainly lay more in the topics discussed thus far than in the political realm. However, in a system where politics avowedly "take command," political deviation of any kind or magnitude may be significant, if not at the moment of indiscretion then perhaps in the future. It is in this light, as a background to the more dramatic events of 1966–67, that we shall consider two episodes which have certainly been recorded by the Chinese leadership as relevant entries in *Chung-kuo Ch'ing-nien*'s political history.

One of these incidents, the second in point of time, occurred in December 1964. The painting on the back cover of *Chung-kuo Ch'ing-nien*'s last issue of the year (Number 24, December 16) was a camouflaged attack on the leadership. On the surface a typical exercise in socialist realism, depicting a team of peasants harvesting grain, the painting in fact carried numerous anti-Mao symbols. Chinese characters vaguely formed in the foreground stubble could be read as "Kill Mao Tse-tung" and "Long Live Chiang Kai-shek"; in the background, one of a group of three red flags (symbolic of the then-current "three red banners" slogan) had fallen to the ground; the peasants were striding forward gaily but not following the lead of a shadowy and dejected figure at the head of their line. Although the message was not obvious there can be little doubt about its deliberateness.

Initially, the authorities acknowledged the attack by trying to recall copies of the number in question. The incident had been publicized abroad, however, by the Canadian correspondent Charles Taylor; and eventually the Chinese simply tried to bluff their way through. The matter was not mentioned in the Chinese press, nor was any evidence of criticism or punishment of anyone concerned ever made public. The painter, Li Tse-hao, was even reported to be continuing his work. The fact remains that someone on the editorial staff of the magazine was guilty of either conspiracy or gross negligence in accepting the painting. An investigation of the magazine's staff certainly followed, but there is no way of knowing what the investigation revealed and what action was taken as a result. The incident must nonetheless have raised questions about *Chung-kuo Ch'ing-nien*'s political reliability.

The other episode in which the magazine's political stand may have become an issue was the Hundred Flowers campaign of 1957. Although the magazine was not singled out for criticism in the "anti-rightist" aftermath of this movement, it is unlikely that it escaped some guilt by association. The damaging associations in question were the journalistic profession as a whole and the Youth League's propaganda system. These groups, like *Chung-kuo Ch'ing-nien*, did not suffer attack as institutions. The CCP was careful throughout 1957 to attack individuals only, without imputing political deviation to any institution or organization as a whole (although it did charge individuals with attempts to take over or establish organizations for their own "rightist" objectives). Nevertheless, there was a sufficient concentration of "rightists" in these fields to assume that more general suspicions were raised and that *Chung-kuo Ch'ing-nien* could not have stayed out of the struggle.

Although no simple description does justice to the events of 1957, we shall try to outline those features of the period that are most relevant to the present discussion.[41] The first point to emphasize is that the revela-

---

[41] For general documentation and analysis of this period, see Roderick MacFarquhar, *The Hundred Flowers Campaign and the Chinese Intellectuals* (New York, 1960).

tions of the Hundred Flowers and Anti-Rightist campaigns were of two different kinds. First, there were accusations by the authorities about the existence of "rightist" or "anti-Party" elements in various places; second, there were accusations by the "rightists" about deficiencies in the existing system. Both kinds of revelations appeared among journalists and the League propaganda network, and both are of interest because they show that the communications system was at once a source of opposition to the CCP and an object of attack by these opponents. On balance, the Youth League and the main official publications were more objects of "rightist" attacks than sources or instigators of anti-regime criticism. The League was repeatedly assailed as a privileged, bureaucratic organization, totally lacking in independence and existing only as a servant of the Party. Official publications were characterized as dull mouthpieces of the regime, suffering from excessive restrictions and obstructions in reporting.[42] The major conclusion to be drawn from the charges and countercharges of 1957 is that Party control of the League and the communications system was sufficiently tight to arouse serious resentment among some people who had contact with these institutions.

Nevertheless, one must not overlook the fact that a significant amount of "rightist" criticism came from within these institutions. Among the newspapers, *Kuang-ming Jih-pao* in Peking and *Wen Hui Pao* in Shanghai were, according to later CCP rejoinders, veritable strongholds of "rightist" thought.[43] "Rightists" in the League were less prominent but still contributed a good share of the criticism of the CYL and its relations with the CCP. Significantly, the main concentration of opposition within the League seemed to be in its publications staff, primarily on *Chung-kuo Ch'ing-nien Pao*. A summary of the charges against these critics will reveal the seriousness of their political errors.

On July 9, 1957, the editorial board of *Chung-kuo Ch'ing-nien Pao* published, in its own paper, a "preliminary investigation" of "bourgeois and rightist" thought on its staff which had caused "big errors" in its propaganda work.[44] Singled out first were editors Liu Pin-yen and Ch'en Po-hung who had published a "harmful and reactionary" article describing the current cultural and artistic scene in Shanghai as worse than under the Kuomintang. Three reporters had written an "anarchistic" article advocating doing away with Party leadership, and a fourth reporter was criticized for a "one-sided" piece he had written. The editors criticized themselves for an earlier editorial which had denied there were actually "rightists" among students and for not taking seriously *Jen-min Jih-pao*'s criticism of *Wen Hui Pao*. They also confessed to having used some of

---

[42] For illustrations, see *ibid.*, pp. 61–76, 93, 100, 109, 121, 123, 132–37, 171–73.
[43] See *ibid.* and the materials in *Hsin-hua Pan-yüeh K'an* (New China Semimonthly), No. 14 (1957), pp. 120–26, and No. 15 (1957), pp. 199–201.
[44] *Hsin-hua Pan-yüeh K'an,* No. 15 (1957), pp. 193–95.

the "rightist" vocabulary. The source of all these errors, said the editors, was "bourgeois and rightist" thought among staff members. Editor-in-Chief Chang Li-ch'ün was guilty of such thoughts, and so was Wang Ya-sheng, deputy director of the reporters' section. On July 18, the newspaper continued its criticism of Liu Pin-yen, who had joined the CCP in 1944 and, "despite help," had never reformed.[45] Liu had attacked the CYL and its cadres, belittling League accomplishments, yet had wanted to make a "second Party" out of it by giving it the character and duties of the CCP and the government.

Jen-min Jih-pao joined in with an article on August 29 attacking Ch'en Hsü-tsung, who until June 1955 had been a member of the NDYL Central Committee and Director of *Chung-kuo Ch'ing-nien Pao*.[46] He lost his positions at that time due to his connections with the "counter-revolutionary" Hu Feng group and had continued to defend his wife who had received a prison sentence for "counter-revolutionary" activities. *Jen-min Jih-pao* did not mention any specific errors by Ch'en during or after his tenure as Director of the newspaper, but the implication was that he represented past weaknesses on its staff and that he might have retained some influence within it.

The climax came in a *Chung-kuo Ch'ing-nien Pao* article of September 21 attacking Ch'en Mo, a member of the CYL Central Committee and Deputy Editor-in-Chief of the newspaper.[47] Ch'en's exposure was said to be a "great victory" in the CYL's (not just the newspaper's) "anti-rightist" struggle; only repeated meetings of the editorial staff and the Standing Committee of the League Central Committee had brought his errors into the open. Ch'en had been a Party member for 19 years but had never overcome his "bourgeois and individualist" ideas. He ridiculed CYL achievements and the Central Committee's leadership of its publications, despite the fact that the Central Committee had strengthened is leadership over the newspaper and increased its circulation from over 100,000 to over 400,000 during the previous two years. Ch'en Mo's main error, however, was his defense of "rightists" in the face of League struggle against them. He used his high position on the newspaper to support the "anti-Party" articles of people like Wang Ya-sheng.

Chinese Youth Press, the publisher and distributor of League publications, also had political difficulties at this time. A *Chung-kuo Ch'ing-nien Pao* article of September 24 attacked Li K'ang, a former Vice Director and Editor-in-Chief of the Press, as the "behind-the-scenes director" of a "rightist " group in the Press.[48] Li, who had been a Party member for over 20 years, had already left the Press for the Central Art Academy

---

[45] *Ibid.*, pp. 195–99.
[46] *Ibid.*, No. 21 (1957), pp. 37–40.
[47] *Ibid.*
[48] *Ibid.*, No. 20 (1957), pp. 98–99.

when the Hundred Flowers campaign began, but he maintained his contacts to lead "anti-Party" activities within the Press. It was his wish to restore "bourgeois freedom of the press" in China and to manage a new youth magazine which would "play counterpoint" to *Chung-kuo Ch'ing-nien.* He argued that cadres in political work did not understand professional matters or intellectuals, and that his transfer out of the Press was a "sectarian incident" perpetrated by the Party.

Among Li K'ang's followers on the Press, of whom four were mentioned, the most important was P'eng Tzu-kang. P'eng was on the editorial committee of *Wen Hui Pao* and was Editor-in-Chief of *Lü-hsing-chia* (Traveller), a CYL geography journal. She tried to make this journal her own "rightist" publication and had solicited articles from leading Party opponents such as Ch'u An-p'ing. Over the previous two years, she had dismissed two-thirds of the Party members on her staff. P'eng said that the CYL Propaganda Department must not control her journal, which she used to oppose the League Central Committee and the Chinese Youth Press and to smear socialism, the Party and the People's Liberation Army. Generally, this group under Li K'ang's influence charged that political work in the publications field was "too left" and that the CYL Central Committee was incapable of leading publications work. They also attacked a number of Party policies over the preceding years.[49]

Allowing for considerable distortion or slanting in these official condemnations, it is still clear that some very prominent staff members of CYL publications committed serious political errors in 1957 and, in some cases, in earlier periods as well. It is equally evident that *Chung-kuo Ch'ing-nien Pao* was the main target of attack when the CCP struck back at its critics. But two questions remain unanswered: Was *Chung-kuo Ch'ing-nien* also guilty of harboring "rightists"? And did the Anti-Rightist campaign raise doubts about the political reliability of the CYL and its leading publications as such? We may give a speculative but affirmative answer to the first question. The absence of public criticism of *Chung-kuo Ch'ing-nien's* staff is more likely to be evidence of its lower status than of political purity. No doubt the worst culprits, from the CCP's point of view, were on *Chung-kuo Ch'ing-nien Pao,* and hence the public display of the struggle against them. But their crimes were probably seen as greater because their positions, on the newspaper and in the Party and League hierarchy, were higher. People residing in China at the time report that the magazine, too, carried out struggles against "rightists" on its staff. Moreover, as we shall argue later in this paper, *Chung-kuo Ch'ing-nien* displayed in 1956 many of the "liberal" trends which would have made it vulnerable to criticism in the struggle that followed the Hundred Flowers campaign.

---

[49] Details on P'eng Tzu-kang's errors are in *ibid.,* No. 19 (1957), pp. 115–16.

The second question also calls for an affirmative answer, although the evidence is only suggestive. The CYL responded quickly to the Party's closure of debate in June 1957 by launching a thorough investigation of its organization. The investigation obviously uncovered serious weaknesses. On August 2, 1957, *Chung-kuo Ch'ing-nien Pao* reported the existence of "rightists" within the League, a situation which had caused some League branches to collapse.[50] As the investigation continued and the Anti-Rightist campaign turned back toward rectification again, the League organized top-level conferences and sent leading cadres on inspection trips to promote internal reform. The Central Committee reorganized some central organs with a reduction of personnel, suspended League schools for a year and reassigned the teachers to manual labor, and sent large numbers of central-level cadres to work in rural areas for "comparatively long" periods.[51] In November 1957, the CYL Central Committee acknowledged a tendency among some League members and youth to ignore politics, a tendency which was incompatible with the "present political situation" and the tasks of the League as a whole.[52] The same directive stated, in what was apparently a cryptic reference to political deviation on the staff of League publications, that the CYL had already strengthened its leadership over *Chung-kuo Ch'ing-nien Pao* and *Chung-kuo Ch'ing-nien* in order to improve their work.

To sum up this discussion, the CYL and its leading publications had acquired by 1957 an image of subservience to, and domination by, the League and Party Central Committees. From a lower-level perspective, nothing that happened in 1957 altered this image. In fact, the leadership's response to the Hundred Flowers campaign was to strengthen central controls over official publications and lower levels of organization, and to remove from office those who opposed this trend. On the other hand, the leadership became aware in 1957 of certain political problems within the CYL and its publications. Specifically, these were resentment within the League about its subservience to the Party, a belief among some "professional" cadres in the publications field that rigid political controls were damaging the quality and effectiveness of publications, and some currents of general dissatisfaction with official policy among youth and youth organizations. The Party made no concessions to these pressures at the time, but rather stepped up its efforts to overcome them. Nevertheless, the seeds of doubt had been planted in the minds of those Party leaders who were determined to persevere in the construction of a Maoist-style Communist society. Although the major campaigns to revolutionize Chinese youth were not to unfold for a few more years, the basis for a new

---

[50] Cited in MacFarquhar, *op. cit.*, pp. 171–72.

[51] *JMJP,* October 30, 1957.

[52] "Directive on Strengthening Reporting, Reading and Distribution Work of League Newspapers and Periodicals," *op. cit.*

sense of urgency about the future attitudes of youth was laid in 1957. The reaction to "bourgeois" professionals and intellectuals was clearer and more immediate. From 1957 on, the CCP was to display a pronounced suspicion of cultural and intellectual circles.

These shifts were to have a significant impact on *Chung-kuo Ch'ing-nien*. Its responsibilities in the realm of political education increased greatly as the Party's demands to revolutionize youth intensified. At the same time, as a journal which in fact aimed largely at the more literate and educated youth and received most of its direction from central propaganda organs, it became ever more closely identified with Peking cultural and propaganda circles—circles which either were suspect by definition since 1957 or were to become the first main targets of the Cultural Revolution. When *Chung-kuo Ch'ing-nien* held a party on October 18, 1963, to celebrate its fortieth anniversary, the festivities were attended by many representatives of "Peking cultural circles." [53] However logical this association might have been in terms of the magazine's role, it was to be a serious political liability in 1966.

---

[53] *JMJP*, October 20, 1963.

III
Content Analysis

The discussion thus far has concentrated mainly on formal problems related to *Chung-kuo Ch'ing-nien*'s organization and role. We turn now to an examination of the magazine's performance and the substantive issues with which it has been concerned. The contents of five different periods in the magazine's post-1949 history serve as the principal basis for this examination. These periods are the first six months (January through June) of 1951, 1956, 1959, 1962 and 1965. The choice of dates is arbitrary, the main purpose being to select periods which represent different moods in Chinese politics without being totally dominated by one particular political campaign. Analysis of the contents should reveal the major substantive issues of each period and show how the treatment of different themes has varied over time.

The content analysis applied here is qualitative rather than quantitative. Although different types of articles have been sorted out and counted in some cases, the sorting and classification is too imprecise to justify presentation of results in numerical form. The analysis relies mainly on important articles, editorials and debates over letters to support conclusions about the general weighting of contents in different periods.

No systematic effort has been made to check the wording and timing of *Chung-kuo Ch'ing-nien*'s contents against higher-level policy statements. The search for delay and variation in official communications is, of course, one of the reasons for employing content analysis; it may reveal significant divisions or shifts in a political system which frequently tries to conceal such phenomena. However, there is no reason to suppose that *Chung-kuo Ch'ing-nien* would be very useful in this regard. For one thing, it is *Chung-kuo Ch'ing-nien Pao,* rather than the magazine, which is the authoritative journal of the CYL and which would be a much more useful gauge for locating political conflict within the League or between the League and higher authorities. Moreover, study of *Chung-kuo Ch'ing-nien*'s contents indicates that the magazine has in fact been a very reliable mouthpiece for the official propaganda line. That is, the contents almost always follow the current line of a given period, or else fall within the tolerated limits of variation and delay for a semi-monthly magazine of its kind. Careful study might reveal exceptions, but in all probability the issue in question would have been brought to light earlier and in more significant form elsewhere.

Chung-kuo Ch'ing-nien does, of course, share responsibility for publicizing those events or new policies which the regime wishes to communicate to the masses. As a result, the magazine serves to some extent as a documentary record of official policy and reaction.[54] Again, however, there are other publications which give a more thorough and authoritative record of official stance. The magazine's most valuable characteristic, which is the focus of interest here, is its presentation in popular terms of the values and behavior which the regime wants youth to observe and its attempt to respond to problems which may obstruct this process. We shall explore this subject by reviewing the contents of each of the periods studied and then by analyzing general trends and variations over the years between 1951 and 1965.

1951

In 1951, as in every other year studied, most of the contents of *Chung-kuo Ch'ing-nien* consisted of articles dealing explicitly with current youth work. Such articles fall into three general types: current policy—the description of current policy and discussions of how and why to implement it; organizational—discussion of organizational and administrative problems in youth work; and ideological—discussion of both abstract theory and the proper approach to "study" and "work style." In 1951, there were several articles of each type in every issue, with the organizational and ideological types being most numerous. Long articles and editorials were relatively scarce, the preferred format being a short article of one or two pages or a brief comment or vignette less than a page in length. Most materials on current youth work were simple, serious and humorless; they made their point in an obvious way with a great deal of repetition in both style and substance. All of these traits are generally characteristic of *Chung-kuo Ch'ing-nien* and need not be noted again.

The most striking feature of the 1951 period was the dominance of a single central theme: the integration of Chinese nationalism and commitment to socialism. This theme was developed most fully through propaganda on the Resist America–Aid Korea campaign, which the magazine emphasized more than any other current movement, and a number of articles discussing patriotism and patriotic education. Materials on Chinese history, anti-American and anti-imperialist propaganda, and articles dealing with the international "peace" movement also contributed to the discussion. Five of the twelve issues focused on topics related to this theme and its presence was evident in every issue. It is not surprising that

---

[54] During the Korean War, for example, the UN Forces' recapture of Seoul after their initial retreat from the Chinese and the failure of Chinese counterattacks in April–May 1951 plainly led to a Chinese reassessment of the likely duration of the war. In the latter part of April, *Chung-kuo Ch'ing-nien* began to comment that some war propaganda was too superficial, was exaggerating American weakness and was producing "false confidence" among the masses; the magazine's first major emphasis on the campaign for "voluntary" contributions from the people to purchase guns and airplanes came in an editorial on June 16.

the Korean War should produce appeals to patriotism and ample material for propagandizing the spirit of collective sacrifice. What is significant in this message is the insistence that patriotism as such—love for one's country and willingness to sacrifice for it—can be, and must be, combined with support for the socialist system.[55] Respect for China and the glory of its past is good; it is in fact insufficiently developed, due to "imperialist suppression," and must be deliberately encouraged. At the same time, it must be raised to a new level by an additional commitment to the socialist future in both the national and international realms.

The other major movements in progress in 1951—suppression of counter-revolutionaries, and land reform—received much less attention in the youth magazine. Articles on land reform were, for the most part, routinely descriptive, perhaps indicating a realistic awareness that most readers were not deeply involved in that campaign. Suppression of counter-revolutionaries was a more prominent subject, but the emphasis was mainly on encouraging a resolute rejection of one's friends and relatives who were so classified. The elevation of the "new patriotism" issue over these two campaigns suggests that the leadership was not particularly worried about youthful support for its basic policies. What it was concerned about was whether this support came solely from the proven appeal of nationalism—a willingness on the part of youth to support any progressive government actively committed to national regeneration—or whether it also came from a real acceptance of the socialist future. The assertion that it must come from both was the primary message of the period.

Chung-kuo Ch'ing-nien's handling of youth problems in 1951 leaves one with a mixed impression. On the one hand, the magazine responded forthrightly to a number of rather technical organizational problems. Questions relating to League admissions, transfer of membership from one branch to another, when to invoke League punishment against members and how severe it should be, and how to handle Party members within the League who were not performing their duties, to cite a few examples, were published and answered in a concrete and reasonable way. These were no doubt very real problems to local League cadres, and the magazine performed a useful service in responding to them. On the other hand, *Chung-kuo Ch'ing-nien*'s treatment of more abstract and personal questions was not very illuminating. The best example is a series of letters on the subject of how a League member could maintain contact with the masses. The exchange began with a letter (No. 56, January 13, p. 46) raising this issue, together with an editorial comment on its importance, calling for further discussion. The debate dragged on, some readers saying that they found it difficult to keep in touch with the masses, others saying that a League member must do so because the masses are

<hr>

[55] For important examples of this theme, see No. 56 (January 13), pp. 10–16; No. 58 (February 15), pp. 15–19; and No. 65 (May 19), pp. 4–5, 14.

the "movers of history." When the topic was concluded with an article on June 2 (No. 66, pp. 8–10), the genuineness of the problem and the doctrinal reasons for overcoming it were clear, yet little had been said about concrete personal motives and responses. The implication was that the principle was important and that once it had been truly accepted, correct action would follow automatically.

A similar conception apparently affected the choice of "models and heroes" during this period. There was no shortage of biographical materials, but they had little direct relevance to the life-situation of most Chinese youth. Articles on the past acivities of Jen Pi-shih, who had died in October 1950, and Mao Tse-tung appeared at the rate of about one per issue, and there was a five-part series on the life of Engels. Lesser figures selected for emulation and honor were mostly "martyrs" who had sacrificed their lives in the Korean War, the war against Japan, or in earlier revolutionary activity. The choice of such illustrious and heroic models is understandable, and may well have had some effect in establishing the ideal of revolutionary accomplishment and sacrifice. It was nonetheless a romantic choice which provided little practical guidance for most of the magazine's readers.

The general tone of *Chung-kuo Ch'ing-nien* in 1951 was, therefore, one of national mobilization and sacrifice, approached with an optimistic and romantic spirit. There was great hostility toward China's domestic and foreign enemies and little room for individual expression or criticism. In fact, there was virtually no significant criticism in 1951, except for occasional attacks on individual cadres who had abused their authority (particularly with reference to the Marriage Law). The only statements about individualism were reminders that collective interests must take precedence. Nonetheless, the magazine's approach to these issues was not at all repressive. The basic assumption was the optimistic one that China's real enemies were few and that the need for their defeat would be obvious to all patriotic Chinese; almost everyone, it was assumed, including those who came from a reactionary class origin, would join in the national effort and would eventually accept the socialist system. Statements about admission to the League, and the carrying on of patriotic education, made it clear that a youth who came from a reactionary class, or who was not yet fully committed to socialism, was not to be treated as an enemy. If he separated himself sharply from the real enemies, he was to be tolerated and encouraged; he was one of the "people" and would respond to education. The possibility that "education" might not overcome all personal conflicts with the political system was not foreseen. The problem as perceived in 1951 was that many youths wanted to work for socialist construction but did not yet understand fully what was required. Once they grasped and consciously accepted the principles—as the Party was confident they would—they would fulfill their revolutionary potential.

The 1956 contents of *Chung-kuo Ch'ing-nien* are more interesting and provocative than those of any other period studied. They are also the most diffuse and difficult to summarize. One could say that 1956 was a period of "liberalization," but such a statement sheds little light on the substance of the issues that appeared in the magazine at this time. We shall discuss here five points which, taken as a whole, give a general image of the period even though none of them actually dominated it.

First

In 1956 the magazine reduced its preoccupation with current youth work and tasks. This general category necessarily remained large, but there were fewer articles dealing with current policy and organizational problems, while those dealing with ideological problems were less abstract. The trend was toward a more realistic recognition and confrontation of the everyday problems of youth. One sign of this was a change in the treatment of models. There were no biographical series on leading Chinese Communists and no real efforts to publicize heroic or romantic martyrs. Models presented were, for the most part, ordinary people or cadres engaged in ordinary tasks. Another sign of the shift was the increased space devoted to readers' letters and discussions of them. In fact, debates centered on letters became the magazine's most prominent method for trying to come to grips with some of the real conflicts that Chinese youth were facing.

A discussion of whether or not youth could be excused for being discontented with rural work is an excellent example, partly because it was the main such exchange in 1956 and partly because it contrasts with the 1951 debate (discussed above) on a related issue. The debate began with a letter from one Li Nan-feng and an editorial appeal for reader response (No. 1, January 1, pp. 16–18). Li stated that many young people were dissatisfied with work in rural towns and villages. More provocatively, he added that this was not a problem of "standpoint" or "philosophy of life" (the standard doctrinal answer to such complaints) but simply an "objective" evaluation of their circumstances. He then cited a number of reasons for what he obviously regarded as justifiable discontent, among them the following: youths coming from cities, where the standard of living is improving rapidly, have a right to expect improvements in village life as well since the aim of communism is a better life for all; since many youths in the countryside are living away from their homes and customary conditions, which most rural cadres are not, they must be excused for feeling homesick; village life is in fact unhygienic and urban youths are right in calling attention to it and demanding rapid change; rural cadres are frequently not sufficiently advanced and do not provide good education for those beneath them, hence it is difficult for youths to improve themselves in rural work; the government has not done enough for the villages in providing improvements in transportation and communications, but rather seems to have devoted most of its attention to improvements in the cities; most youths going to the countryside are males and cannot find wives there.

Publication of reader response began two issues later. The editors stated they were receiving over two hundred letters a day on the subject, the "great majority" disagreeing with Li; they announced they would print only letters of disagreement since Li's point of view had already been expressed. The letters published, although critical of Li's conclusions, did not deny that many of the conditions he described existed. Generally, they emphasized the necessity for some personal sacrifice and argued that improvements in rural life would result from urban youth's work in the countryside but could not realistically be a pre-condition for it. The debate concluded, after a reported 8,000 letters had been received, with an article on April 16 (No. 8, pp. 2–7). The article was predictably an uncompromising refutation of Li's argument, stressing the need for struggling against obstacles and having faith in the revolutionary future. Still, it maintained the realistic tone of the exchange by observing that the villages were indeed backward and would remain so until the growth of industry and culture in the cities laid the foundation for their modernization. Chinese cities are backward, too, said the author, and they must retain priority in development for some time to come; to talk of urban-rural equality now is foolish. While this conclusion may not have persuaded Li Nan-feng and his supporters (and we must remember that he did receive support although it was not published), he had obviously touched off a serious public discussion—and received a serious answer—on a question of immediate importance to Chinese youth. There were many other discussions, such as whether one ought to follow a cadre's order when one is convinced it is unsound (conclusion: obey the order but petition for reconsideration) and how children of bourgeois families will be affected by socialist reform (conclusion: their standard of living will be lowered but their political status will be improved by removal of the class stigma), which reflected an equally deliberate appraisal of genuine conflicts arising in Chinese society.

Second

The 1956 period included a large number of articles on the question of individualism and individual interests. As the Li Nan-feng debate illustrated, the supremacy of collective interests remained official doctrine. Other articles made the same point, notably one on the new selective military service system (No. 1, January 1, pp. 12–13, 31) which criticized those youths who were not eager to serve, or who liked service for "selfish" reasons—such as a desire for a good life or personal honor. However, while *Chung-kuo Ch'ing-nien* continued to stress the principle of personal sacrifice for the national cause, it also tacitly recognized (as indeed the article on military service had) the existence of substantial misgivings about or violation of this principle. The majority of articles on this subject clustered around the question of whether it was a sign of "individualism" or "individual heroism"—pejorative terms which had been freely applied—for one to pursue private hobbies and interests in his spare time, to devote himself to study in an effort to advance his position, or to express his own views in study and discussion. These questions were usually raised by readers who had been criticized for their extra-curricular activities and who felt that cadres were discouraging their hopes for further study and advancement. It is significant that these readers defended themselves publicly and even more significant that the magazine was cautiously receptive to their complaints. The editorial response was that one should never strive for advancement purely for personal reasons and that, from a realistic point of view, one ought not to undertake too many activities or set his sights too high. At the same time, they agreed that cadres should not discourage private interests or hopes for advancement by applying the "individualistist" label. They pointed out that personal advancement was actually consistent with collective interests in view of current national needs.

Third

There was a marked increase in receptiveness to individual expression. The obstacles that over-zealous cadres and rural assignments created for courtship and marriage were considered openly and at times sympathetically. Letters about personal dress established the rule that thrift was a virtue but that individual choice should prevail; colorful dress was not in itself a symbol of "bourgeois" life. The numbers of short stories, songs and poems published in the magazine increased significantly. While emphasizing that art and literature should serve socialism, articles encouraged youth to become artists and writers and to improve their technical skills in these fields.

Fourth

A "march to science" campaign had a major impact on the contents of *Chung-kuo Ch'ing-nien* in 1956. Articles praising science and the pursuit of knowledge appeared in almost every issue. Much of the material devoted to "study," which in other periods normally meant political study and self-cultivation, took on more academic overtones. The value of learning from "old professors" (i.e., bourgeois intellectuals) was recognized. An editorial on May 1 (No. 9, pp. 4–5) put weight behind the campaign by observing that students had a "burden of excessive social work" that was hindering their studies and the march of science. Schools are a place for developing cadres, science, and culture, said the editors: "free" the students and let them study.

Even more striking was an article by Hsiao Wen-hui (No. 5, March 1, pp. 24–25) which put the matter squarely on the line. There are those who believe, Hsiao said, that people who attend meetings and speak regularly in political discussion are participating in politics, while those who do not are "escaping politics." Hsiao stated flatly that this was not true; those who concentrate on their own work are, in fact, fulfilling a primary requirement of socialist construction by marching to science. Next he observed that many cadres believe it is permissible for non-activists to concentrate on academic work but that Party and League members must attend to political work. This is not true either, since Party and League members are the cream of Chinese youth and must contribute their best; if they have a "non-political profession," then they should give it primary attention and reduce their political work. In reality, said Hsiao, it is those who deny these facts who are "escaping politics;" they are old cadres, educated before liberation and recruited during the early campaigns, who do not understand that the political situation has changed and, with it, the primary tasks of youth. In the future, some will still specialize in political work because it is a job that has to be done. Others will do some political work in their spare time. But concentrating on study and the development of science is also a primary demand of the present political situation. Hsiao's views did not represent official policy, of course, but they were not refuted and they were repeated, in less forthright terms, in other articles and letters.

Fifth

Finally, as the preceding discussion suggests, *Chung-kuo Ch'ing-nien* carried a substantial amount of significant criticism during 1956. This criticism was not as sweeping as that which emerged in the Hundred Flowers campaign a year later; that is, it did not attack the existing system as such, either as inherently unsatisfactory or as a perversion of a "true" socialist system. It did, however, go considerably beyond *pro forma* comments that things have been well done but can still be improved, or attacks on individual cadres who had, in presumably exceptional cases, committed errors. Cadres were the main objects of criticism in 1956, but the criticism was frequently cast in general terms suggesting that the error was due to a flaw in the system rather than individual deviation. In addition to charges of suppression of individual initiative, referred to above, there were complaints about bureaucratic behavior, about the use of cadre status for personal gain and advantage, about excessive cadre demands for criticism of oneself or one's colleagues which simply led to fabrications and personal conflicts, and about cadres' lack of interest in youth problems and suggestions. The magazine treated these complaints sympathetically and at times carried cartoons lampooning the behavior in question.

There is no reason to believe that *Chung-kuo Ch'ing-nien*'s 1956 editorial policy was out of step with official policy. The magazine continued to give full support and coverage to the major policies of the period, such as the collectivization of agriculture. When necessary, as in the Li Nan-feng debate, it tried to refute views which were seen as seriously opposed to orthodox policy or values. The new tone of *Chung-kuo Ch'ing-nien* was, therefore, a reflection of a shift in mood at higher levels, a shift which permitted the mass media to become, temporarily, much more re-sponsive to the needs and questions of readers. This mood was still opti-mistic about the basic revolutionary tendency of youth; had it not been so it could not have tolerated such open discussion of dissatisfaction. However, its main feature was a realistic understanding that youth were not to be revolutionized by a romantic gloss which ignored or painted over their misgivings. The mood of 1956 ended a year later when expres-sion of discontent surpassed what the Party regarded as tolerable limits. We may be sure that, despite earlier approval, *Chung-kuo Ch'ing-nien* could not have avoided a critical re-examination of its 1956 editorial policy during the Anti-Rightist campaign of 1957.

1959

The most prominent feature of 1959 was a revival of the emphasis on current youth work and tasks. However, in contrast to 1951 and 1956, the organizational type of article received very little attention. In place of discussion of League organizational and administrative problems there was an overwhelming volume of material on current policies and abstract ideology. Articles on the people's communes and the Great Leap Forward were published in every issue, and these policies were also the real subject of many general discussions of youth work. The ideological emphasis ap-peared most strikingly in a fourteen-part series "Lectures on Socialism and Communism," prepared by the CYL Propaganda Department, which occupied a total of 34 pages—roughly the equivalent of one complete issue of the magazine. This lecture series was in addition to another large group of articles on formal Communist theory.

The relative decline of the League organizational focus did not mean an absence of "officiality." On the contrary, the presence of higher au-thorities was very evident in *Chung-kuo Ch'ing-nien* in 1959. The CYL Propaganda Department contributed separate articles in addition to its lecture series. Prominent national figures, such as Ch'en Yi, T'ao Chu, Hu K'o-shih, Teng Tzu-hui, Hsü T'e-li and Li Ta wrote pieces for the magazine. Moreover, there were again, as in 1951, a number of articles about Party leaders, including six on Mao, four on Liu Shao-ch'i and three on Chou En-lai.

The expression of dissatisfaction that had flourished in 1956 predict-ably disappeared, to be succeeded by a euphoric affirmation of China's progress in socialist construction. The only criticism that appeared was a general chiding of those who were not "leaping forward" fast enough or who expressed "conservative" doubts about China's ability to overcome all obstacles by human effort. The latter issue furnished the substance of the major letter exchanges of the period. Readers who confessed to discouragement about their positions or abilities, or who raised questions about the value of heroic sacrifice, were deluged with exhortations to continue their struggle, have faith in the future and forget their personal ambitions and interests. Actually, these debates were not entirely one-sided, for the editors did give some space to counter-arguments. Although the official response was evident from the first, it is significant that an attempt was made to keep some lines of communication open. In 1959 *Chung-kuo Ch'ing-nien* was not open to criticism of Party policies, but it was interested in discussing some of the personal problems that these policies created.

The blatant romanticism and optimism of 1959 is on the surface reminiscent of 1951, but the similarity is misleading. In retrospect, it is clear that much of the exuberance of 1959 was not only false confidence but even falsified confidence. Even without retrospect, however, one can see crucial differences in the tone of the 1959 and 1951 contents of the magazine. One of these is the overpowering presence and dominance of the Party in the later period. In 1951, there was some sense of distinction and even autonomy about the youth movement. The League was, to be sure, a CCP auxiliary, obligated to assist the Party in its work, but at the same time it had an organizational life of its own which reflected the distinctive problems of young people who were not yet assuming full adult roles in society. With this distinction went a greater tolerance for the gradual development of socialist consciousness among youth. By 1959, however, the Party had increased greatly its leadership over the youth movement in an effort to bring youth directly and totally into the struggle for socialist construction. The Party's tasks were far too urgent to permit youth to stand aside; young people were to take part in productive labor and the war against nature, reform their thoughts immediately, and take the lead in nationwide socialist education.

Another significant difference in 1959 is the appearance of signs of uneasiness about the revolutionary qualities of Chinese youth, although the general theme of reliance on their basic progressiveness remains. A long summary of Mao's ideas on this subject, prepared by the editors of *Chung-kuo Ch'ing-nien* and published on May 1 (No. 9, pp. 2–9), demonstrates the new tone. In statements made during 1957, Mao had made reference to three points which foreshadowed the Party's increasing anxiety about the revolutionization of youth. First, he stated that the real socialist revolution was not simply change in the system of ownership of means of production, which had already taken place, but political and ideological change in man; this implied that the most difficult tasks of the revolutionary period still lay ahead. Second, Mao observed that political and ideological work among youth was in some cases weak; it must be improved so that all youth would attain a correct political standpoint. Finally, he pointed out that some youth lacked social experience and held illusions about an easy life under socialism in which there would be no further need for struggle. These ideas, which may not have received much attention when first expressed, were in 1959 selected by the editors for inclusion among Mao's most important statements about Chinese youth. Moreover, they appeared over and over again in those articles which discussed current ideological work among youth. The romanticism of 1959 tended to obscure the long-range implications of this new attitude toward youth. In fact, the CCP had already ceased to take the revolutionary qualities of youth for granted and had begun a deliberate effort to revolutionize them by a combination of ideological indoctrination and immersion in "revolutionary" struggle.

1962

For *Chung-kuo Ch'ing-nien,* as for China generally, 1962 was a period of difficulty and uncertainty. Both the economic strain and the crisis of confidence which accompanied it were evident in the magazine. The economic setback that followed the Great Leap Forward was probably responsible for a sharp reduction in the size of the magazine. From an average size of about forty pages per issue in earlier periods, it was cut to about twenty-five pages per issue; moreover, there were only ten issues in the first six months of 1962 as numbers were combined on two occasions. The total absence of editorials or reproduction of higher directives presumably reflected uncertainty at higher levels. There was also a noticeable decline in the quality of the magazine's letters-from-readers section. The period failed to produce a single sustained readers' debate and many potentially fruitful questions raised in letters were left dangling without much response.

Despite evidence of political and economic restraints on its contents, *Chung-kuo Ch'ing-nien* continued to transmit the Party's current concerns about the youth movement. Although authoritative clues from editorials and centrally-directed campaigns were absent, the weighting of contents outlined three major themes. One of these was a drive to educate youth in "lofty Communist morality." There was nothing novel about the virtues that this drive extolled. Diligence, thrift, social discipline and dedicated service to society were the main ingredients—all by this time familiar appeals to Chinese youth. However, in the past the CCP had not stressed so explicitly the moral basis of these virtues, but rather had emphasized their instrumental value. For example, thrift was a virtue in the Korean War in order to save money for the war effort, serving the collective interest was in the long run the rational way to advance individual interests, hard work for a few years in the Great Leap would produce a beautiful society in the future, and so forth. These instrumentalist arguments were still used in 1962, and it is obvious that hard times and a threatened breakdown of public order gave the virtues mentioned a very practical justification. Nevertheless, the Party chose in 1962 to define these virtues in moral terms, thereby giving them a universal and permanent value that transcended the current situation. Puritanical and selfless struggle was to be part of every youth's basic character, not just a way out of the "three bad years."

A closely related theme was "cultivation of revolutionary successors." Although that specific slogan was not widely used in 1962 (it was to be most prominent in 1964), the arguments and concerns connected with it were very much in evidence, particularly in discussions of Communist morality.[56] Simply put, the argument stated: first, no one develops Communist morality or revolutionary spirit naturally, even those who are raised in a socialist society or are children of cadres and other "revolutionary" class families; second, the creation of a Communist society will take several generations and will, therefore, fail unless deliberate efforts are made to pass on the revolutionary spirit to each succeeding generation. The reasoning behind these assertions need not concern us here. Developments from 1957 through 1961 certainly offered empirical evidence for both of them; doctrinal explanations cited the influence of bourgeois family backgrounds and "thousands of years of feudalism," plus a dangerous tendency for some cadres and their families to succumb to "bureaucratism," desire for special privilege, and so forth. Whatever the explanation, by 1962 there had been a significant intensification of the CCP's message that youth must revolutionize themselves. In 1959, the uneasiness about this question had remained mainly in discussions on the theoretical plane. Three years later, it had become a demand for Communist education in the family, in the school, and in society at large. Youth must be trained to think and live according to Communist morality and a revolutionary spirit.

The third theme that received considerable attention in 1962 was that cadres must renew their effort to get close to the masses, the specific reference in this case being to League cadres and others with close youth contacts. This was not an extension of the 1959 "mass line" euphoria, which had extolled the limitless power and creativity of mass action. It was instead a reassertion of the more sober aspect of the mass line, which holds that the people must always be consulted to develop popular support by persuasion and to check against bureaucratic errors. Thus, the mass line literature of 1962 had a basically critical attitude toward cadres in the youth movement. The point raised most frequently was that cadres

---

[56] The most authoritative treatment of this subject was an article by Hu K'o-shih in No. 6 (March 16), pp. 2–5. Other good examples are found in Nos. 3–4 (February 5), pp. 24–26 and Nos. 9–10 (May 7), pp. 13–15, 22.

must not regard themselves as "something special," must not avoid contact with the masses outside their official routine; rather they must extend themselves to make friends with non-cadres in order to understand popular problems and needs. Another common point was that cadres must listen to all opinions, however diverse and from whatever source. Though a slow and possibly painful method for cadres, they must stick to it with confidence that it is the best way to resolve problems and to educate all concerned.

An interesting feature of these three themes is that each had both an idealistic and realistic side. That is, although each set a high ideal standard—for Communist morality, perpetuation of the revolutionary spirit, or cadre-mass relations—each also expressed a very somber awareness of the current gap between ideal and reality. The ideal suggested a world of revolutionary struggle and sharp class consciousness, whereas the real world of early 1962, as presented in *Chung-kuo Ch'ing-nien,* was relatively free of either revolution or class struggle. To be sure, doctrinal statements attributed the deficiencies of 1962 to bourgeois, feudal, and revisionist influences, but doctrine was silent on precisely where these influences were to be found in China of 1962 and how they were to be struggled against. By explicit admission, class origin and family background were no guarantee of immunity to reactionary influences. The suspect groups of 1959 (intellectuals, specialists, and children of bourgeois families) not only escaped consistent criticism in 1962 but were accorded a certain amount of recognition for their useful services.

In short, Chinese youth were given a clear message to revolutionize themselves through study, struggle, and self-cultivation. They received, too, a list of the virtues they were to develop and the evils they were to oppose. But the revolutionary struggles in which they were to steel themselves were non-existent, and the evils were pervasive phenomena scattered throughout society without connection to specific classes or social strata. During the Great Leap, revolutionary spirit could be cultivated and used in a struggle against nature and all manifestations of conservative thought. By 1962, however, nature had proved unconquerable and some of the "conservative" notions of 1959 had acquired official sanction. The problem that lay beneath the propaganda appeals of 1962 was how youth were to revolutionize themselves in a non-revolutionary situation.

1965

Chung-kuo Ch'ing-nien's most obvious characteristic in 1965 was the revival of its role as a vigorous propaganda organ. It returned to publication of twelve separate issues for the six-month period and increased its size to about 30–35 pages per issue, still less than in the 1950's but substantially more than in 1962. More significantly, the editorial department of the magazine came out into the open again. Thirteen full-length (two to three-page) editorials, one short editorial and two long articles by the editorial department were published during the period. Finally, the magazine restored its coverage of League organizational problems to a level roughly comparable to 1951 and 1956. It not only printed a large volume of material dealing explicitly with League work but drew heavily on middle-ranking League officials (provincial and municipal League committees and committee members) for reports and articles.

The clarity and focus of propaganda campaigns, which had been absent in 1962, were also restored. In September 1962, the Tenth Plenum of the CCP Central Committee had promised renewed efforts to promote class struggle and socialist education, and by 1965 these efforts had materialized in three main themes that dominated the pages of *Chung-kuo Ch'ing-nien*. One of these was glorification of the thought of Mao Tse-tung, stressing its usefulness in solving problems of any nature and its importance as the guide for all revolutionary action. Another was "serving the poor and lower-middle peasants," a theme which extolled the revolutionary class character of these groups and the ideological value of maintaining close contact with them. For intellectual youth, "serving the peasants" meant respecting them as people, demonstrating personal concern for their problems, and assisting them in education and the acquisition of modern knowledge. The third theme was glorification of physical labor in rural and mountain areas; its slogan was: "one must revolutionize through labor" *(ko-ming-hua chiu tei lao-tung-hua)*. Hard labor in the mountains and villages was not only an essential task of economic construction but also, for intellectual youths, the only way to acquire the "redness" of proletarian experience to go with their "expertness."

Chung-kuo Ch'ing-nien handled these themes seriously. It gave them heavier editorial emphasis than it had given to the major issues of any other period studied. It provided model reports on how they were implemented at the local level and published large numbers of letters bearing individual testimony and experience. It acknowledged no exceptions to, or compromise with, the general principles of accepting Mao's thought, serving the peasants, and universal participation in physical labor. It wove them together into a model image of a militant, active, class-conscious youth, who was trained simultaneously in modern knowledge and physical labor, who despised all forms of privilege, personal ambition, and soft living, and who was prepared to study and follow without question the teachings of Mao Tse-tung. This militant message was amplified by other materials, such as a continuation of the "learn from Lei Feng" campaign, a great deal of support-Vietnam–oppose-American-imperialism propaganda, and much discussion about strengthening the militia and its military training. Thus, the specification of where and how to struggle, which had been missing in 1962, was now supplied, at least at the propaganda level. Whether or not there were real social conditions for a renewal of class conflict and revolutionary struggle in China is, of course, a different question.

Chung-kuo Ch'ing-nien's militancy in 1965 is particularly significant in light of the magazine's suspension in August 1966. If it was actually following the Maoist line so faithfully, why should it have been a casualty of the Cultural Revolution? Was there any evidence in 1965 of tendencies which would have proved politically embarrassing a year later? It is tempting to look for such tendencies in the hope of finding a tangible explanation for the magazine's downfall, but, unfortunately, the search is not very rewarding. There are a few points which deserve mention, however.

First, *Chung-kuo Ch'ing-nien*'s position on the development of revolutionary spirit within the educational system, a question in which it naturally had a deep interest, was "correct" but nonetheless cautious. It supported fully the proposition that all students and intellectuals should be both red and expert, that all those primarily engaged in intellectual work should also engage in physical labor and political activities. It supported, too, the imposition of political qualifications in admission to higher schools, and the absolute priority of state needs in deciding post-graduation assignments. Significantly, however, it gave no indication of a desire for major changes in the existing system, a demand which was to become one of the key issues in the Cultural Revolution. The magazine's position, despite the revolutionary phraseology, was essentially support for the status quo—an educational system that provided institutionalized channels for political activity and periodic physical labor but that did not allow these activities to disrupt the academic process. This position was quite evident in an editorial of April 16 (No. 8, pp. 12–13), which praised the revolutionary campaigns but then added that schools were, after all, a place for study. Students should not neglect their studies, take examinations lightly, or disparage the idea of academic training, said the editors, noting that the emphasis on physical labor and rural service sometimes had this effect; nor should political activities ever become so frequent or demanding that they interfered with study time, rest periods, or the normal operation of the schools. The editors obviously could not have approved the storms that erupted in the schools in June 1966 and that brought formal education in China to a complete halt.

Second, the magazine's policy on League admissions was contrary to the spirit of the Cultural Revolution and the Red Guards on one important point—the attitude toward children from bourgeois, landlord, and rich peasant families. *Chung-kuo Ch'ing-nien* gave full support to the League Central Committee in its insistence that such youths should be admitted, irrespective of their family history and even of their own previous mistakes, if they gave assurance that they were now committed to socialism. The magazine published many letters on this question through-

51

out the first six months of 1965, always stating the policy clearly. There is no doubt that the League's position here could have been interpreted later as being "soft" on class struggle.

Finally, the magazine published one article (No. 4, February 16, pp. 5–7) by the Construction Department of the Peking Municipal Committee of the CYL. As we shall note later, this committee was the only League organization to be prominently denounced and purged during the Cultural Revolution. Among the sins ascribed to it was praising "model" branches which did not give sufficient weight to the thought of Mao Tsetung. The *Chung-kuo Ch'ing-nien* article is a case in point, although it was not the incident held up for criticism later. The main virtue of the League branch praised in this article was that it had overcome existing hostility toward young workers from reactionary families; little emphasis was given to Mao's thought in the article, although there were a few unimportant citations. The magazine also published articles on model branches that did indeed emphasize Mao's thought and that were to receive the stamp of approval in the Cultural Revolution. However, it is possible that even a single error, such as publishing a tainted article from the Peking CYL Committee, could have hurt the magazine.

The fact remains that none of these points, except possibly the publication of the Peking committee article, suggests deliberate opposition on the part of *Chung-kuo Ch'ing-nien*. The magazine was simply following the official propaganda line of the time, taking its cue on certain problems of particular concern to youth from the CYL Central Committee. Its error was not independent opposition but its attempt to pass on faithfully to its readers the policies of its guiding organizations. To place those policies in their proper context and see why they were controversial, we must broaden our examination to include developments in the youth movement generally in the period leading up to the Cultural Revolution. First, however, some concluding comments on *Chung-kuo Ch'ing-nien*'s pre-1966 history are in order.

SUMMARY

As noted in the introduction, the primary function of the mass media in China is the broadly educational one of communicating officially-approved messages and material in order to develop among the people the values and behavior desired by the regime. The mass media also transmit "objective" information and encourage the growth of two-way communications between officials and the public, but their performance of these functions is always subordinate to, and heavily penetrated by, the educational one. Our survey of the contents of *Chung-kuo Ch'ing-nien* in selected periods has illustrated this point. The magazine has grappled sporadically with problems as perceived by youth themselves and has carried a certain amount of basic news and information of interest to its readership. It has tried most consistently and thoroughly, however, to define and structure the role which the CCP wishes youth to assume in Chinese society.

For *Chung-kuo Ch'ing-nien,* the central issue over the years between 1951 and 1965 was how long the "revolutionary" period was to endure and what demands it was to make on Chinese youth. A basic shift in elite expectations on this issue occurred, in approximate terms, in 1956–58. The "approximate" qualification is necessary since the data analyzed here permit neither precise dating of policy changes nor any conclusions about the development of new attitudes among specific groupings within the Chinese leadership. The shift probably took place over a long period of time and had quite different degrees and timing of acceptance among different sections of the leadership. However, the main components of the shift can be described.

Before 1956–58, the CCP anticipated a relatively short and sharp conflict with its class enemies, to be followed by socialist construction, which it perceived largely in institutional terms. The Party demanded ideological reform among the people but assumed it would develop in a relatively harmonious way, through peaceful persuasion and education, in step with institutional changes. Revolution and class struggle were very real, but their targets were mainly clear-cut enemies who were opposed to socialism or who could, by class analysis, be presumed to be opposed; the main exception was a small group of Western-trained intellectuals who were counted among the "people" because of their support for the Party but who also faced intensive ideological remolding because of their heavy exposure to bourgeois influences. The Party appeared confident that socialist construction would take place in a context of basic national unity once the obvious enemies were destroyed.

Chung-kuo Ch'ing-nien's effort in 1951 to make an explicit connection between patriotism and socialism, suggesting that the former was an appropriate point of departure for the creation of socialist consciousness, illustrated these early hopes for broad national unity in the march toward socialism. Significantly, this theme was not continued; there was not a single discussion of the ideological implications of nationalism in any of the later periods studied. Although the CCP continued to capitalize on patriotic feelings, particularly in times of crisis, it did so without suggesting that nationalistic unity was the foundation of the Chinese state. The growing belief among the leadership that revolutionary action and class struggle must continue meant that conflict rather than unity, and class rather than nation, were to be the defining characteristics of Communist China for some time to come.[57]

The shift to which we are referring was, therefore, in simplest terms,

---

[57] See the discussion in Schurmann, *op. cit.,* pp. 115–18.

a new expectation that the revolutionary period would last indefinitely, with all the struggle, conflict, and sacrifice that revolution demands. This shift encompassed at least two steps, both very evident in *Chung-kuo Ch'ing-nien*. The first was a realization that the Chinese "people" would not develop socialist consciousness quickly or easily, even when the institutional establishment of socialism was complete. In 1956, on the assumption that the revolutionary period was ending and that the universal growth of socialist consciousness had begun, the CCP had begun to relax its controls over communications, permitting a fuller expression of opinions, problems, and criticisms. This trend was not simply an imitation of de-Stalinization in the Soviet Union nor was it a product of the "Hundred Flowers" slogans, for it antedated both. The relaxation reached its peak in the spring of 1957, but it had then been in progress for over a year. The point is that the "liberalization" of 1956–57 was the beginning of a long-term trend which was consistent with the Party's early optimism about the rapid conclusion of the revolutionary period. The trend was reversed, of course, in June 1957, but it was reversed only with what must have been a profound sense of disillusionment with the meager results of the Party's efforts in the ideological field.

The first reverse step, then, was an insistence that the real revolutionary task was the ideological struggle to create socialist man, a struggle which institutional reform had manifestly not resolved. However, in the early part of the Great Leap Forward, the leadership still seemed to believe that this task, difficult as it was, could nonetheless be accomplished in one generation by prodigious efforts to indoctrinate and mobilize the population. The second step, which completed the shift, was the realization that several generations of struggle would be necessary to carry out the revolution. Some signs of this belief were evident in *Chung-kuo Ch'ing-nien* in 1959; by 1962, after the failure of the Great Leap Forward and the emergence of Soviet "revisionism," it was a dominant theme.

The change in Party expectations about the revolution had a profound impact on the Chinese youth movement. Up through 1956, the political role of Chinese youth was not a salient national issue. The regime was preoccupied with the destruction of the old system, and a series of campaigns against what it regarded as its primary enemies. It took youthful support in these struggles largely for granted, provided only that youth study and organize under proper leadership. As a result, the youth movement had a certain degree of autonomy. Although it was exposed to, and expected to respond to, national issues in a prescribed way, the League and its publications were also free to devote a good deal of attention to problems of concern to youth and the League but not directly relevant to national politics. By 1959, the combination of anxiety about youth's shortcomings and the hope that they would nonetheless lead the revolutionary effort had made the youth movement as such a macropolitical issue. Literally everything that happened within it was either a response to initiative from higher authorities or else was vulnerable to doctrinal evaluation and interpretation in terms of central policy demands.

The way in which *Chung-kuo Ch'ing-nien* transmitted to its readers the CCP's growing concern about their revolutionary quality has already been described. A related question is how this trend affected the magazine's performance of its multiple roles. Obviously *Chung-kuo Ch'ing-nien* has been most consistently a Party propaganda journal—the role that in practice has been the easiest and safest to fulfill and that has corresponded most closely to its public image. In two of the periods studied—1959 and 1962—the magazine was almost wholly devoted to exposition of the official propaganda line. Nevertheless, it would be wrong to conclude that the magazine's other formal roles have no substance.

In 1951 and even more in 1956, *Chung-kuo Ch'ing-nien* was in part a general youth magazine. There were in the former period a significant number of articles on Chinese history, different regions and resources of China, and various aspects of life in the Soviet Union, which presented informative general knowledge even though their contents supported current propaganda themes. The editorial tone of the magazine was light compared to later years. Editorials were very short, and the editors engaged in both self-criticism and informal commentary in which they wrote freely about complaints received and how they were responding to them. The magazine did not, in fact, probe personal problems very deeply, but it gave the impression of being genuinely open to its readers' interests and questions.

It was in 1956 that *Chung-kuo Ch'ing-nien* achieved its best balance among its assigned roles, devoting almost equal attention to official propaganda, general youth problems, and League problems. Although articles on the Soviet Union were already tapering off (in 1956 such articles numbered about one-third what they had been in 1951; in 1959 there were only five, in 1962 none, and in 1965 only critical references), there was a wide scattering of information on other countries, including some non-Communist ones. The publication of poetry, fiction and song was at its peak in 1956, as was the amount of critical and penetrating discussion of youth problems. Perhaps the most striking sign of the magazine's service to its readership was its coverage of educational and academic subjects. Partly this was due to the "march to science" materials, representing an official campaign, but there was also descriptive discussion of scientific and technical subjects for their own sake. The year 1956 was the only one studied of which this can be said. In other periods, articles on science and technology were either doctrinally oriented (e.g., on the "red and expert" problem or general praise of modernity and scientism in a socialist society) or else they were confined to a few prominent examples of applied science (most commonly, personal health and hygiene,

55

agricultural technology, and public sanitation). It is conceivable that in 1956 a Chinese student might have read *Chung-kuo Ch'ing-nien* for *pleasure*—a most unlikely event at any other time. In any case, the general interest content of the magazine fell off sharply in 1959, 1962, and 1965. One could find at most only a handful of articles in any of these periods offering general information on subjects other than Party doctrine and policy and League affairs.

Chung-kuo Ch'ing-nien's performance as an official organ for the League followed a similar pattern. It filled this role best in 1951 and 1956, and then tended to downplay it in 1959 and 1962; however, in contrast to the general youth magazine role, the League role was very prominent again in 1965. One measure of this pattern is the volume of editorials and documents on League affairs, which declined steadily from 1951 through 1962. There were fourteen editorials in 1951, six in 1956, one in 1959 and none in 1962; similarly, several League Central Committee directives were printed in 1951, a few in 1956, and none in 1959 and 1962, although the CYL Propaganda Department contributed a large volume of doctrinal argument in 1959. Routine documentation is not in itself a particularly good measure, of course, since *Chung-kuo Ch'ing-nien Pao* assumed major responsibility for this after 1951. On the other hand, *Chung-kuo Ch'ing-nien*'s general treatment of League affairs and organizational problems, in the form of articles and reader-editor exchanges, followed closely the editorial and documentation pattern. This was true in the revival of 1965 as well, for the sixteen editorials and editorial articles that appeared in that period were accompanied by numerous reports on CYL affairs from various League committees. Actually, the 1965 volume of editorials and high-level League reports exceeded that of 1951, since the editorials and directives printed in the earlier year were normally very short.

From these comments, it is clear that the CCP's post-1956 elevation of youth problems to the national policy level had a pronounced impact on *Chung-kuo Ch'ing-nien*. Although the magazine was never formally relieved of its other duties, it became in practice a mouthpiece of the CCP's propaganda network. It would be a mistake, however, to read into this development any conclusions about inevitable or irreversible tendencies toward the stifling of communications media in China. While the function of the communications system plainly makes it susceptible to rigid content control from above and to lack of responsiveness to lower levels, this fact has not prevented *Chung-kuo Ch'ing-nien* from filling a more open, varied, and responsive role at certain times. It could presumably do so again if the Party's obsessive concern about revolutionizing youth were to slacken.

Three additional points deserve mention in concluding this summary. First, one must remember that *Chung-kuo Ch'ing-nien*'s readership consists mainly of more literate youth, of whom the great majority are probably students or cadres in contact with students. Its message aims at a broader audience, since the magazine is to furnish guidance and material for cadres and activists who work with youth not counted as direct readers. Nevertheless, in the absence of empirical confirmation of how the message is transmitted to non-readers, it is safest to assume that the magazine's greatest influence is on the more literate and highly educated portion of the young population and that the problems it reflects are also essentially problems of this group.

Second, while keeping the above limitation in mind, the power and intensity of *Chung-kuo Ch'ing-nien*'s message in the post-1956 years must have had some effect on Chinese youth. There is no way for an outsider to measure this effect, but some of the relevant considerations are evident. On the negative side, there is the twin problem of disbelief and loss of interest that heavy-handed propaganda always risks. If a reader's image of reality does not support what he reads, he may cease to believe what he sees in a journal like *Chung-kuo Ch'ing-nien;* or, even if he believes, he may simply cease to take seriously what is presented in such monotonous and doctrinal terms. Even more powerful resistance may be generated by perceived conflicts between the official line and a reader's personal interests and values. The whole point of the campaign to revolutionize youth is an open acknowledgment of the presence of such factors.

There are equally significant points, however, on the positive side. Although the intensity and totality of the message are relatively new, the language and symbols are not. The "goodness" of revolution, struggle, and sacrifice, and the "badness" of personal interests, soft living, and bourgeois influences, are well established stereotypes in Communist China. One cannot dismiss as meaningless appeals to symbols which have been defined so clearly, even when the appeals may be repetitive and obscure from an objective point of view. Moreover, the appeals are directed at youth, presented in idealistic terms, and graced by the personal blessing of a man with awesome national presitge. While these conditions cannot guarantee universal responsiveness among youth, it is likely that those at the most impressionable ages will respond with the most unreserved energy.

Finally, there is the overall impact of the communications system which has, since the Great Leap, steadily focused ever sharper attention on the fundamental issue of how to keep China "red." As information on other subjects and issues has decreased, both the relative and absolute salience of this issue have been raised. There is no point in speculating on how youth might respond if they had a more varied flow of information. The fact is that youth in China have been deprived of information not only about the outside world but even about their own country. Their attention has increasingly been directed toward domestic issues, presented in crisis terms but with only a minimum of hard information to back up moralistic and doctrinal exhortations. In such circumstances, youth may well respond positively and genuinely, and even emotionally, to issues that in other times and places would have little appeal. To repeat, *Chung-kuo Ch'ing-nien* tells us only the message and not how it is received. But there is good reason to believe that the message may have had a significant influence on the values and behavior of many Chinese young people.

Third, the 1965 revival of *Chung-kuo Ch'ing-nien*'s editorial assertiveness and emphasis on League affairs commands special attention. From one point of view, it is evidence of the magazine's ability to alter its style in the midst of a long-term trend toward more rigid and uniform control of communications. As such, it supports the earlier suggestion that the reduction of *Chung-kuo Ch'ing-nien* to a Party propaganda organ was not irreversible. More significantly, perhaps, it raises the question of why the magazine should have moved in this direction. The move was plainly not a return to the more open stance of 1956 or even 1951, since the heavy-handed doctrinal approach of later years was retained and even heightened. Nor was the move in "opposition" to the then current line, for *Chung-kuo Ch'ing-nien* remained energetically articulate in its support for the campaigns of that time. In all probability, *Chung-kuo Ch'ing-nien*'s 1965 performance was a function of new assertiveness by the CYL, passed on to the magazine presumably with the approval of the Party Propaganda Department. Again, however, this raises questions which must be placed in a broader context.

IV
The Great Cultural Revolution

The CYL and its main publications were among the major casualties of the earlier phases of the Great Proletarian Cultural Revolution. Although the full story of their downfall remains unknown, we can outline roughly the relevant events and the possibly damaging associations of the CYL leadership. These associations are particularly significant because there have been virtually no high-level public attacks on the League or its publications. The outline must, therefore, include some reference to the Cultural Revolution itself.

The movement began in the fall of 1965, following a special meeting of the CCP Central Committee in which Mao Tse-tung apparently declared his intention to push the campaign against bourgeois and revisionist influences to a new peak. This campaign had actually been in progress since the latter part of 1962, operating under various names and from time to time shifting its focus of attack. On the propaganda level, it had been pushed vigorously. Mao believed, however, that it had not been pushed hard enough in practice, and that both domestic and international threats to his vision of China's future were greater than ever before. The first step was an attack on a small group of men in the cultural and educational field. The "bourgeois" ideas and "anti-Party" activities of these men soon became symbols that had to be rejected decisively by all who were to stand on the Maoist side. In the spring of 1966 the struggle intensified. By June, several important figures and groups had been identified, allegedly by their failure to support the campaign against the bourgeois "black gang," as reactionary opponents to Mao's brand of socialism. Among the major groups criticized, all of them to be partially reorganized, were: the CCP Peking Municipal Committee, headed by P'eng Chen; the CCP Propaganda Department and several leading figures in cultural and educational circles; and the Peking Municipal Committee of the CYL.

It is difficult to imagine a constellation of groups more closely associated with *Chung-kuo Ch'ing-nien* or, in view of the seriousness of the charges, more dangerous to it. After these accusations and purges, the magazine could not have avoided some self-criticism and explicit repudiation of what had been its leading organizations. Among *Chung-kuo Ch'ing-nien*'s direct superiors, only the CYL Central Committee remained untarnished, and for a few more weeks it appeared that the League might weather the storm. Criticism of the CYL Peking Committee carefully absolved the League Central Committee by listing among the former's

59

crimes several instances of violation or disregard of directives from the latter. The first meeting of the new, reorganized CYL Peking Committee (July 3–11) was called under the "direct leadership of the CCP Peking Municipal Committee [now also reorganized] and the CYL Central Committee," and included Hu K'o-shih of the League Central Committee as a main spokesman. All was not well with the League, however. First Secretary Hu Yao-pang had disappeared from the news early in the year. At the July 3–11 meeting, there were references to a need for "reorganization" of the League to bring out its "militant core." Nevertheless, whatever its shortcomings, the CYL continued to speak of its present and future tasks as though it had no doubts about its survival, and on July 25 *Chung-kuo Ch'ing-nien Pao* announced that it would soon begin publication six times a week.[58]

For the CYL the critical development was the Eleventh Plenum of the CCP Central Committee, held in Peking from August 1–12, 1966. The Plenum released two major documents, neither of which made any reference to the CYL although both paid tribute to the importance of "revolutionary" youth. On August 18 came the first massive Red Guard rally in Peking. Thereafter, the League simply disappeared, while Red Guard units became the dominant and approved form of youth organization. *Chung-kuo Ch'ing-nien* was published on schedule on August 1, but its next issue of August 15 never appeared; *Chung-kuo Ch'ing-nien Pao* published its last issue on August 19.

The significance of the Eleventh Plenum emerged gradually during subsequent months. During June and July, Mao and his "close comrade in arms" Lin Piao had tried to extend the Cultural Revolution into a mass movement that would search out all traces of bourgeois "cultural" influence. The universities became the main arena of struggle and were thoroughly disrupted, but many high-level cadres tried to check the scope and intensity of the campaign. The Mao-Lin group responded to this resistance at the Eleventh Plenum by citing as the "main targets" of the movement "those within the Party who are in authority and are taking the capitalist road." These authorities included a large number of top Party officials, headed by Liu Shao-ch'i and Teng Hsiao-p'ing. Thus, with the Eleventh Plenum, the Cultural Revolution turned into a bitter struggle for power between the Mao-Lin group and much of the established leadership of the state and Party bureaucracy. The League and its publications were apparently among the first victims of this new phase not because they had overtly opposed Mao but because their past policy and organizational associations with the Liu-Teng group were so close.

Developments since August 1966 confirm this impression that the CYL is a secondary target of the Cultural Revolution. The League has ceased

---

[58] See *CKCNP*, June 23, 1966, in *SCMP*, No. 3735 (July 11, 1966); and *CK CNP*, July 26, 1966, in *SCMP*, No. 3756 (August 9, 1966).

functioning and has received a good deal of criticism at the local level. It obviously cannot revive under the present power structure without a thorough purge and reorganization. On the other hand, the Mao-Lin group has followed what must be a deliberate policy of refraining from public attacks against it, and has thereby kept open the possibility that it may be revived in the future. Occasional references to the League during the first months of 1967 suggested that it still existed, at least on paper, and that some of its cadres who were actually "good or comparatively good" had been unjustly criticized at earlier points in the movement.[59] It appears that the attachments of the CYL and its publications to the Liu-Teng group forced their suspension as a defensive move, but, once neutralized, they could be left waiting without public attack until the major struggle was settled.

There is a paradox in the fate of the CYL and its publications that mirrors a similar problem in the convulsions that have shaken the Party leadership during the Cultural Revolution. The paradox is that the violence that has characterized the methods and language of the campaign seems to be incommensurate with the actual severity of the crimes committed by its opponents. Thus, the performance of the League may have deviated on some points from a pure Maoist line, but scarcely so far as to justify not only its suspension but also the eruption of violence against League cadres and between rival youth groups. So, too, at the central leadership level there were policy differences between the Mao-Lin group, but these hardly seem to merit a confrontation that would tear the Party apart and bring China perilously close to civil war. A full discussion of this question is not possible here, but our analysis of *Chung-kuo Ch'ing-nien* has raised several points which suggest that serious frustrations and resentments within the youth movement may have exacerbated the character of the Cultural Revolution. Although these points relate specifically to the youth movement alone, we must remember that youth and the policies that concern them have been at the core of the campaign.

First, the actions of the Red Guards are generally consistent with the Party's propaganda line over the last several years. In retrospect it is evident that neither the League nor many top Party leaders, including the CCP Propaganda Department itself, wished to see a literal realization of the "revolutionization" of Chinese youth. Revolutionary thought and action, if they are to have any meaning, must find definable objects of attack among established social patterns. The League and Party leader-

---

[59] For example, see "Cadres Must Be Treated Correctly," *Hung Ch'i* (Red Flag) editorial, No. 4 (1967), in American Consulate General (Hong Kong), *Selections from China Mainland Magazines* [hereafter cited as *SCMM*], No. 566 (March 6, 1967); and other articles on the cadre question in *Hung Ch'i,* No. 5 (1967), in *SCMM,* No. 571 (April 10, 1967).

ship were understandably reluctant to be too specific about the institutions to be changed by the revolutionary fervor they were cultivating. They were particularly careful to avoid any suggestion that the CYL, the CCP, the educational system, or the general economic system established in the wake of the Great Leap's failure were to be disrupted by rapid and radical changes. Unfortunately for them, they were to be the victims of their own closed communications system, for it proved to be extremely difficult to give the revolutionary message top propaganda priority and yet simultaneously set forth the limits of revolutionary action. To have done this openly would have compromised both the message and the integrity of the communications system. To do so implicitly and by occasional warnings not to carry the revolution too far or too fast, which was generally the course followed, risked underplaying the need for restraint and exposing to attack the very institutions they wished to protect.

Whatever the intent of the leadership, they had for several years been exhorting youth to rebel, to struggle, to fear no sacrifice, to recognize and expose bourgeois and revisionist influences throughout society, and, above all, to take their stand on revolutionary and moral principles regardless of who might oppose them. It would be foolish to argue that Red Guard actions were totally spontaneous or were motivated entirely by these revolutionary values. On the other hand, the revolutionary message probably contributed significantly to the willingness of some youths to rebel against their local authorities and rival groups even at the risk of physical conflict. Earlier generations of youth, they knew, had displayed their virtue in anti-imperialist strikes, in the Long March, against the Japanese, in Land Reform, and in the Korean War, while their own "revolutionary" acts seemed limited to winning ping pong tournaments, increasing production, living in deprived areas, and so forth. Many youths may have longed for a "real" revolution in which to demonstrate their commitment to Maoism.

Second, the CYL's recruitment campaign of 1965 was, in a sense, a preview of the Red Guard movement of 1966 and a harbinger of some of the sharp conflicts within the League that the latter raised. As noted earlier, CYL membership began to stagnate about 1959, eventually leading to a forceful recruitment effort in 1965. The quality and distribution of League membership had been a matter of concern ever since the early 1950's. Although total membership grew rapidly from 1949 through 1959, capitalizing on the large pool of eligible but unorganized youth, the pattern of recruitment was never wholly satisfactory. Three deficiencies were common subjects of discussion. One was bureaucratism and inferior political standards among some members and cadres, probably an inevitable result of the NDYL's rapid expansion after 1949. The Hundred Flowers and Anti-Rightist campaigns of 1957 produced considerable evidence on this point. Another League deficiency was the distribution, by class background or current assignment, of the membership. The League was strong in schools, government enterprises and the army, but relatively weak in rural areas.[60] Finally, the League had an excessive number of over-age members. Out of a 1957 membership of 23 million, 2.8 million were over 25 (the regular upper age limit) and one million of these were over 28 (the acceptable extension limit). Most of the over-age members were certainly cadres, and hence very difficult to dismiss. Moreover, it was recognized at the time that the problem would worsen in the future as large numbers would reach the upper age limit each year.[61]

None of these problems were solved in the years between 1957 and 1964. In the aftermath of the Hundred Flowers experience, and with the tougher class line that accompanied the Great Leap, the CYL tried to tighten up on the political credentials of its members. The net effect, however, was apparently to reduce admissions without materially improving the League's performance. By the crisis year of 1962, *Chung-kuo Ch'ing-nien* materials on "getting close to the masses" indicate that the CYL was facing a serious problem of separation from youth. Sporadic references to new recruitment were not supported by official figures on increased national membership. By 1964, CYL membership in proportion to the eligible population had almost certainly declined, and the organization was less and less representative of the group it was supposed to organize and lead.[62] At the same time, Party pressure was building up through the "cultivation of revolutionary successors" campaign to proceed rapidly

---

[60] In 1957, out of a total membership of 23 million, 16.4 million were in villages, 3.6 million in schools, 2.28 million in industry, 1.8 million in the army, 970,000 in government offices and 680,000 in commerce; see *JMJP,* May 15, 1957, cited in *CNA,* No. 633. Since the figures total over 25.7 million, it appears that a substantial number of rural members were serving in the other capacities mentioned. The League made no secret of the fact that its organizational work was weakest among the peasantry.

[61] Lo I, "Kuan-yü Chung-kuo Kung-ch'an-chu-i Ch'ing-nien T'uan Chang-ch'eng (Ts'ao-an) ti Pao-kao" (Report on the CYL Regulations, Draft), in *Hsin-hua Pan-yüeh K'an,* No. 12 (June 25, 1957), pp. 69–72.

[62] In 1957 the League said its membership was 19.17 per cent of the total youth population. There are no reliable figures for either CYL membership or the youth population in 1965. However, if we assume League membership to be 25 million, then the total youth population would have to be 130 million or less to maintain the 19 per cent figure. A 130 million estimate for the 15–25 age group is obtained only when one uses the very lowest estimate (715 million) for the 1965 population of China; see Aird, *op. cit.,* pp. 363, 365. In all probability, the age group was something over 130 million in 1965. Demographic factors may have a direct bearing on League membership problems. It appears that those becoming fifteen years of age in the years between 1959 and 1964 were few relative to both earlier and later periods; those turning fifteen after 1964 are much more numerous as a result of the population explosion following 1949. Chinese demography could thus partially account for both the recruitment problem of 1959–64 and for the incentive and success in the 1965 campaign. See Aird; and S. Chandrasekhar, *China's Population: Census and Vital Statistics,* 2nd ed. (Hong Kong, 1960), p. 47.

and thoroughly with the drive to revolutionize youth.[63] The League was called on for a supremely important effort at a time when it was organizationally at low ebb and increasingly "non-revolutionary" in quality.

A *Chung-kuo Ch'ing-nien Pao* editorial of April 2, 1964, laid out the CYL's task, and by implication its crisis, in no uncertain terms.[64] The League had to expand its organization and increase its fighting power, particularly in rural areas where members constituted only 13 per cent of the rural young population (much below the national membership as a percentage of all youth—see note 62); about 10 per cent of rural production teams had no CYL members and about 30 per cent had only one or two. Another problem, the editorial continued, was over-age members. The League faced either an absolute decline in membership or transformation into a "league for middle-aged people" unless it promptly took in young recruits who would create a "new atmosphere" and a "new leadership core." Specifically, the CYL was to concentrate on recruiting youth under 20, particularly those in the 15–18 age bracket; it was urged to give first priority to recruitment in the countryside, and, in the cities, to focus on the middle schools. In stressing the importance of "cultivating successors" at an early impressionable age and of injecting enthusiastic new blood into the League, the editorial hinted at the existence of conservative, bureaucratic opposition from CYL cadres. There must have been some resistance since the campaign did not get underway for another year, despite its manifest urgency.

On February 18, 1966, the New China News Agency announced that the CYL had recruited 8.5 million new members in 1965, the highest number ever enrolled in one year.[65] The figure is extraordinary and possibly represents a loose and exaggerated estimate. There is no reason to doubt, however, that a massive inflow of new members occurred, a fact that makes all the more remarkable the League's disappearance within the year. Two points are particularly important in assessing this campaign. First, it suggests that a major effort was made to push the CYL in the direction the Red Guards were later to follow. Recruitment efforts focused on peasant and worker youths under twenty, many of whom had had no previous political experience.[66] There was a definite "rectification" air to the campaign, with many references to over-age cadres being removed, bureaucratic restrictions and resistance being overcome, and

---

[63] For important articles on this 1964 campaign, see *Training Successors for the Revolution Is the Party's Strategic Task* (Peking, 1965). See also Hu Yao-pang's report to the CYL Ninth Congress in June 1964, and the *JMJP* editorial of July 8, 1964, both in *CB*, No. 738.

[64] *SCMP*, No. 3208 (April 29, 1964).

[65] *SCMP*, No. 3646 (February 28, 1966).

[66] *CKCNP* carried details and editorials on recruitment throughout the fall of 1965. See *SCMP*, No. 3547 (September 29, 1965), No. 3554 (October 8, 1965), No. 3561 (October 20, 1965), No. 3564 (October 25, 1965), and No. 3607 (December 30, 1965).

elections putting young and untried men into basic-level cadre positions. The average age of both members and cadres was reduced in many branches. Reports emphasized that new recruits would bring a fresh, revolutionary quality to an organization that was displaying signs of obsolescence, even though they might make a few mistakes. Thus, from this perspective, the recruitment campaign appears to have been an attempt to transform the League into an organization that could fill the role later filled by the Red Guards.

There was another side to the movement, however, that spelled failure for any attempt to change radically the character of the League. For one thing, the League deliberately allowed and encouraged children of "bad" family origin to join. The Second Plenum of the CYL Central Committee (March 29–April 19, 1965) upheld the line of "uniting with and organizing the absolute majority of youth," a line which stated that "over 95 per cent of youth, including the great majority of sons and daughters of the exploiting classes, are demanding advance and have an active revolutionary spirit." [67] The liberality of this dictum became more evident as recruitment progressed. Youth need not be "perfect" but only "good in the main." Even if they had committed mistakes or had serious defects, they could be admitted if they indicated they would try to reform. The League was plainly out to get new members, quickly and in quantity, and it was not too particular about their qualifications. The precise results of this approach are obscure but it definitely lessened the supposed emphasis on admission of truly "revolutionary" youth. The February 18 announcement was less than enthusiastic about the qualities of the new recruits. It said only that "many" of them were activists, that "most" had high class consciousness and revolutionary vigor, and that "some" youth of exploiting families had been admitted. No doubt the League took in many youths who were excellent Red Guard material, but it apparently admitted along with them large numbers of youths who were to be objects of Red Guard attacks.

Moreover, the promised rejuvenation of cadre ranks was in practice only a partial victory. Reports recognized the prevalence of powerful vested interests and conservatism among cadres. Vague but revealing references were made to senior cadres who did not trust young people, who had argued for "consolidation" rather than expansion of membership, who had placed severe restrictions on admission in the past and who had blocked advancement of cadres beneath them. The campaign supposedly "broke the convention of attaching importance to qualifications, seniority, and grade." Despite such strong words, however, the cadre structure apparently resisted a thoroughgoing rejuvenation. Examples indicated that most of those who were promoted to positions of responsi-

[67] Text of the Ninth Plenum's Communique is in *CKCN*, No. 10 (May 16, 1965), pp. 2–3. See other articles on this theme in *ibid.*, pp. 4–5, 9–10.

bility were already serving as cadres; they were not truly inexperienced and untried. In any case, the League made it clear that new cadres were not to be given a free hand. Their promotions were essential for the "revolutionary cause," but they would still have to accept guidance and education from older cadres before they would become acceptable leaders.[68]

This discussion points to an interesting dualism in the idea of cultivating revolutionary successors. The Party has presented the slogan as a simple implementation of Mao's thought, as a truly revolutionary movement. In fact, however, the slogan is open to two interpretations. One emphasizes the word "revolutionary" and refers to the recruitment of cadres who possess Maoist attributes. The other emphasizes the word "cultivation" and refers to the necessity of providing adequate training and guidance in the development of leadership material; it can in fact be made to justify the routinization of bureaucratic training and promotion. In the case of the CYL recruitment campaign, both interpretations were present but it was the latter one which apparently guided the action of senior cadres. It is very possible that a similar dualism, and a similar choice of priorities, prevailed in the Party and state bureaucracy in their handling of this issue. If so, it helps to explain how the future opponents of the Cultural Revolution could have deviated significantly from Mao's wishes even when they were accepting and promoting his slogans.

To summarize, the CYL tried in 1965 to reverse a trend that was leading to its obsolescence as an instrument of Maoist policy. Through its recruitment campaign, it tried to re-establish its strength and its claim to monopolize the organization of Chinese youth. Its efforts were substantial and brought a new assertiveness to League work; as we have noted, *Chung-kuo Ch'ing-nien* reflected this assertiveness in its editorial policy.[69] Ultimately, however, it could not or did not go far enough to win Mao's confidence. In relaxing admission standards and stopping short of a real rejuvenation of its leadership, it reaffirmed its identification with the prevailing policy of the Liu-Teng leadership group and forfeited its last opportunity to serve as Mao's agent for revolutionizing youth. When the leadership split became open in August 1966, the CYL was simply replaced as an organizational weapon by the *ad hoc* organization of Red Guards. Perhaps the recruitment drive accomplished something, however,

---

[68] *CKCNP*'s discussion of this point was a less than graceful acceptance of "revolutionary" priorities. In answering the question of whether it was "unfair" to promote young cadres who were "slightly inferior" to comrades who joined the revolution before them, it said this was indeed "unfair." However, "fairness" is "disadvantageous to the revolutionary cause"; one must appreciate the "strategic significance" of Mao's instructions on cultivating revolutionary successors. *CKCNP*, editorial, December 11, 1965, in *SCMP*, No. 3607.

[69] *CKCN* also tried to increase its readership and distribution in the countryside during the recruitment campaign. See *CNA*, No. 633, p. 6.

for it did mobilize large numbers of youth who had previously been kept out of organized political activities and it did give official sanction to the airing of long-standing conflicts between senior and junior levels of the youth movement. It is possible that some of the newly admitted youth constituted a readily available core for the formation of Red Guard units. This possibility would partly account for the rapid emergence of the Red Guards and also for Mao's reluctance to attack publicly the CYL as a whole.

A third point that our analysis of *Chung-kuo Ch'ing-nien* has shown to be a central issue in the youth movement is the CCP's policy of "revolutionizing" the educational system. The general thrust of the policy has already been identified as an attempt to combine sound academic training with physical labor, ideological indoctrination, and a "class line" favoring the admission of children from "revolutionary" family backgrounds. The policy was developed after 1957, was relaxed in 1961–62, and then was reasserted after the CCP's Tenth Plenum in the fall of 1962. In June 1964, the Ministry of Education released new regulations on the admission of students to institutions of higher education that called for state-established quotas and admission based on examination of political thought, academic qualifications, and health.[70] The examination of political thought gave officials power to implement the "class line," which had been intensified after 1962. The result has been increasing tension among students and among all organizations concerned with the formal educational process.

The most obvious aspect of this educational policy is the threat it poses to academic standards and to those who wish to pursue academic and professional careers. It has undoubtedly been resented and even resisted by many people whose study and work lie in these areas. It is particularly frustrating, of course, for those who come from a "bad" family background and feel that their advancement, both within the schools and in future assignments, is jeopardized by factors beyond their control. Less obvious perhaps, but no less real, is frustration felt by those who are on paper the beneficiaries of the policy but who have not in fact felt its full benefits. Despite official favoritism toward children of worker and peasant backgrounds, they have not secured proportional representation in institutions of higher education. Although they constitute about 90 per cent of the young population, their percentage of national college enrollment, according to official figures, has risen slowly from 20 per cent in 1952–53, to 48 per cent in 1958, and to 66 per cent in 1965; some observers believe the last figure should be only 50–55 per cent.[71] There have

---

70 NCNA, June 3, 1964, in *SCMP*, No. 3234 (June 9, 1964).

71 See *Peking Review*, No. 12 (1958), p. 16; A. S. Chang, "Education," in Kirby, ed., *op. cit.*, pp. 83–84; and Leo A. Orleans, "Communist China's Education: Policies, Problems and Prospects," *An Economic Profile of Mainland China*, Vol. II, p. 504.

been times, as in 1961–62, when the percentage actually dropped; it is also probably lower in the better universities in the major cities and lower among graduating classes than among college students as a whole. By a very crude estimate, based on the most favorable 66 per cent figure for 1965, about 3 per cent of youth from exploiting families attend college as against only .5 per cent from worker and peasant families.

The causes of this discrepancy lie mainly in the basic cultural and motivational advantages of children of the existing intellectual elite. So long as aptitude and examination results have any meaning, as they have even under the "class line" policy, children of "bad" origin will gain more than their proportionate share of college places. What concerns us here are the consequences. In effect, the policy has created conditions for very widespread frustration among students who aspire to higher education. Those from exploiting families will resent official bias against them, a bias which always threatens to deprive them of the fruits of their academic advantage. Those from worker and peasant families will resent the state's failure to fulfill its promise to reduce dramatically the high proportion of students from "landlord and bourgeois" families. This situation has surely produced hostility between the two types of students and grievances against school authorities from both of them. The results have been evident in the violence and virulence of student activities in the Cultural Revolution, and in the frequent Red Guard accusation that school authorities have discriminated against students of worker and peasant origin.[72]

An equally important consequence has been the strain placed on organizations and officials concerned with educational problems. In the aftermath of the educational disruption of 1966 and the Mao-Lin-Red Guard attacks on high-level cadres in the cultural and educational field, it is evident that many officials believed CCP educational policy was unrealistic. They supported it fully on the surface, and perhaps accepted its ultimate objectives, but they were determined to pursue it in a moderate way which would not disrupt the flow or quality of graduates.[73] This approach was exposed and repudiated in the spring of 1966. Among those who favored it was the CYL. *Chung-kuo Ch'ing-nien*'s insistence in 1965 on the importance of study and academic standards has already been noted. *Chung-kuo Ch'ing-nien Pao* went even further in an editorial of August 29, 1965, which might almost be regarded as a classic of "revisionism" in its field.[74] The editorial not only upheld the importance of study but insisted that it must follow from "voluntariness" and "self-awakening" and that it must be flexibly adjusted to individual interests and

---

[72] For a good sample, see "Five Red Guard Leaflets," *CNA*, No. 636 (November 11, 1966).
[73] See "Education, 'Bourgeois' or Proletarian?," *CNA*, No. 617 (June 24, 1966).
[74] *SCMP*, No. 3541 (September 21, 1965).

requirements, whatever they might be, so that individual specialities could be developed. Statements of this kind plainly differed from the Mao-Lin line of organizing all study around politics and the works of Mao Tse-tung. There is evidence to suggest that the CYL was forced to repudiate its position by publishing on September 7, 1965, a document that had been adopted at its Second Plenum in March–April but not made public then; the resolution acknowledged League shortcomings and reaffirmed its task of organizing youth for the study of Mao's thoughts.[75]

It is not surprising, therefore, that the Cultural Revolution found some of its most explosive fuel in the educational field. The CCP's educational policy had generated both personal resentments and policy differences that turned quickly to bitter struggle under Mao's pressure for a final victory. The conflict is not over yet, however. The League and its publications would not have followed the line they did without confidence that they spoke for a powerful opinion; the Red Guards would not have reacted so violently without some sense of injury and frustration. The effort to implement the revolutionary line within the schools has produced controversies that will dominate youth affairs for some time to come.

Underlying all of these points is the question of what the future holds for Chinese youth. For several years now the answer has been a life of struggle, sacrifice and physical labor. Probably no fact of life is more important to youth, in terms of their personal ambitions and concerns, than the fact that the overwhelming majority face long-term or permament assignments in rural or isolated areas. For peasant youths, who are the great majority, there may be nothing particularly severe about this prospect. For those who reach middle school, however, and are exposed to urban life and the hopes of higher education, a wider range of alternatives and ambitions has been unveiled. Unfortunately for them, the opportunities for higher education and urban assignment are sharply limited. Only about one out of six junior middle school students goes on to senior middle school.[76] In the early 1950's most senior middle school graduates could enter college, but this situation changed as higher educational facilities reached their limits and the CCP began to encourage rural work assignments for middle school graduates. Higher educational enrollment reached a peak in 1960–61 but then declined.[77] In 1964, only 1.3 per cent of college-age youth were attending institutions of higher education.[78] Exactly what proportion of middle school and college graduates remains in urban areas is not clear, but it is certain that the pressure to go to rural

---

[75] See *CNA*, No. 633. Text of the resolution is in *SCMP*, No. 3542 (September 22, 1965).

[76] Orleans, *op. cit.*, p. 508.

[77] *Ibid*, pp. 509–10.

[78] *CKCNP*, August 13, 1964, in Chang, *op. cit.*, p. 91.

areas applies to this group as well as to the overwhelming majority that never reaches even this educational level.

Economic and demographic imperatives may explain the sharp restrictions on higher education and urban assignment but do not necessarily make them more palatable to youth. The Party's glorification of physical labor and serving the peasants, so amply documented in *Chung-kuo Ch'ing-nien,* is evidence of the basic unpopularity of rural assignment. Scattered reports suggest that some young people who had been sent to villages and border areas took advantage of the disruption caused by the Cultural Revolution to return to the cities.[79] Exhortation and indoctrination may reduce resistance to rural assignments, but in trying to eradicate it the drive to revolutionize youth has set itself an unattainable goal. Although this problem has not been a direct issue in the Cultural Revolution, it has probably contributed to the general frustrations among youth, which have added to the violence and confusion of the campaign. Like the educational issue, this fundamental limitation on the career prospects of Chinese youth cannot be resolved by the Cultural Revolution.

Despite its ambiguities and inconclusiveness, the Cultural Revolution offers some important insights into the effort to revolutionize Chinese youth. It has demonstrated that the cumulative effect of CCP propaganda is significant, that it has inspired many youth to rebel against what they believe to be evil influences and practices in the Chinese system. In doing this in the face of physical threats and conflicting appeals, they have shown a degree of politicization which testifies to the power of the Party's message. The Cultural Revolution also demonstrates that in recent years the Chinese leadership has been much less successful in fixing the concrete targets of political action than in communicating the value of political action. The reason for this is the basic contradiction inherent in trying to revolutionize a society through the medium of estabished institutions. For a time the contradiction was submerged by a *de facto* softening of the revolutionary message into a call for reform and social service. The bureaucrats who directed the main institutions could do little else, for a true revolution would ultimately have to find its enemies among them. Hence, when Mao and his supporters decided that moderation was in the long-run equivalent to reaction, much of the institutional structure could not or would not carry out his demands. Without unified organizational guidance, the Cultural Revolution disintegrated into turmoil and confusion.

Nowhere was this confusion more evident than among youth. Although they were more willing than any other group to respond to Mao's call, their regular organization and communications media had been suspended. Without their customary leadership, they quickly demonstrated

---

[79] See *CNA,* No. 654 (April 7, 1967), pp. 3–4; and *Current Scene,* 5:2 (January 31, 1967), p. 8.

that there was no real consensus among youth about the objectives or targets of the campaign. Some attacked their "authorities" while others defended them. Some of their actions received central approval and some did not. Rival groups sprang up, struggled with each other, were merged and disbanded, all under the rubric of carrying out the revolution. Through it all, there were signs of some legitimate grievances and complaints, but no clear program around which a stable majority could unite.[80] "Revolution" simply did not make sense when put to the test of practice, for it threatened to destroy the very organizational network that had for so many years promoted it.

The Maoists profess to be satisfied with the role of youth in the Cultural Revolution. They claim that vast numbers of "revolutionary successors" have now emerged from the turmoil, tested and steeled by their living experience of "class struggle."[81] The Maoists may well believe this claim, for they obviously regard the training aspect of the Cultural Revolution as one of its major justifications. However, the struggle thus far has been too confused and uncertain in its consequences for anyone to specify with confidence what youth were struggling for and what experience they might have gained. No doubt the early stages of Red Guard activities elicited an intense revolutionary fervor, but this fervor may now be fading, and even turning toward cynicism or despair with the Maoists' inability to consummate their revolution. The longer it takes to produce tangible accomplishments, the greater the danger that youth will lose sight of or relinquish the ideals that mobilized them for action. Whether this danger is averted or not, China's present and future leaders must come to terms with the sobering fact that many Chinese youth have revolted against what they believe to be the deficiencies of their political system—and may do so again.

---

[80] One of the best descriptions of this aspect of the Cultural Revolution is the series of articles by Andrew Watson on events in Sian, in *Far Eastern Economic Review,* 56:3, 4, 5, 7, 8 (April 20–May 25, 1967).

[81] Lin Chieh, "Courageously Forging Ahead in the Teeth of Great Storms of Class Struggle," *Hung Ch'i,* No. 5 (1967), in *SCMM,* No. 571 (April 10, 1967).